W.H. Strobridge

Catalogue of a valuable collection of coins and medals

made by an amateur and now the property of Loring G. Parmelee

W.H. Strobridge

Catalogue of a valuable collection of coins and medals
made by an amateur and now the property of Loring G. Parmelee

ISBN/EAN: 9783741139604

Manufactured in Europe, USA, Canada, Australia, Japa

Cover: Foto ©ninafisch / pixelio.de

Manufactured and distributed by brebook publishing software (www.brebook.com)

W.H. Strobridge

Catalogue of a valuable collection of coins and medals

CATALOGUE

OF A

Valuable Collection of Coins and Medals,

MADE BY AN AMATEUR,
(J. Carson Brevoort)
AND NOW THE PROPERTY OF

LORING G. PARMELEE, Esq., OF BOSTON, MASS.

With an Important Addenda,

BELONGING TO

J. AUGUSTUS JOHNSON, Esq.,
(LATE U. S. CONSUL GEN. FOR SYRIA.)

THE WHOLE TO BE SOLD BY AUCTION

AT

Clinton Hall, New York,

BY

THE MESSRS. LEAVITT, AUCTIONEERS,

ON THE

AFTERNOONS OF JUNE 12th,

AND FOLLOWING DAYS,

Commencing Monday at Half-past Two o'clock, and continuing each Day at the same hour until the end of the Week.

CATALOGUE BY WILLIAM H. STROBRIDGE.

1876.

INTRODUCTION.

There is in almost every collection of coins, a particular class upon which the possessor has bestowed more than ordinary pains—some department in which he takes more than a general interest. It is only by patiently waiting for opportunities to secure the best out of many such collections that a cabinet like the one described in this catalogue can be formed : for the quality of its various elements is undoubtedly up to the highest standard, and every department appears to have enjoyed the maker's partial favor.

It is for this reason that the present catalogue is likely to receive a cordial welcome at the hands of a large number of persons interested in coins. It is not alone the collector of the coins and medals of England and Scotland—of fine American coins—of the rare and expensive political medals and tokens of our own country—of our costly Colonial series—of fine and rare historical coins and medals—or the lover of that higher branch of pure Numismatics—ancient coins—that may expect to find something here to his taste. In this catalogue is much that cannot fail to suit the wants and requirements of ALL CLASSES of advanced collectors, and it is this consciousness that has made its preparation a pleasant task. It would be useless to deny that under other circumstances such work would become monotonous; to enumerate and describe, day after day, objects in which the writer feels no *especial* interest, needs the assurance that his labor will be appreciated by *amateurs*, to keep it above the level of literary drudgery.

But these remarks hardly apply to this particular catalogue. It is but the truth to say that no other collection of coins and medals has given the writer more satisfaction and enjoyment from first to last in his various relations to and dealings with it than this.

It was formed by an amateur and scholar whose industry in his pursuit, and knowledge of coins, were simply wonderful. When compelled by a partial loss of sight to give it up, it was transferred to another *amateur*, who being willing to invest a fortune in coins, is certainly entitled to his lustre.

By far the larger part of the original collection, with important additions from Mr. Parmelee's own cabinet, is now offered for sale. Nothing out of the American department has been changed, and the changes that have been made, although resulting in gain to the new possessor, have hardly been attended with loss to the collection, when due credit is allowed for the additions.

I cannot dismiss the subject without speaking once more of the *varied* as well as *excellent* character of the coins and medals which this catalogue comprises.

The extraordinary quality of the colonial department (although by no means large), is fully equalled by that of the series of U. S. cents, and these in their turn deserve no higher praise than to be favorably compared with the Washington series, and that of Political Medals and Tokens. The silver coins and patterns, struck at the National Mint, would make an ordinary sale attractive, and yet it is doubtful whether these will command more admiration than the really excellent division appropriated to the English series.

The ADDENDA is another property. It is the collection of J. Augustus Johnson, Esq., gathered by him while he was United States Consul-General for Syria, with his residence at Beyrout. It will be found highly interesting and novel, especially as to the numerous Jewish coins, and the pretty little silver pennies struck by the Princes of the Crusades.

I hope the catalogue will receive the compliment of a thorough examination, and that its defects will either be overlooked or forgiven. I might rather almost venture to invite *criticism*, in view of the valuable assistance that my friends, Messrs. Balmano and James, have, with such great disinterestedness, given me. This public acknowledgment of their services is the least return that I could make, yet it is far more than their modesty would permit them to ask.

W. H. STROBRIDGE.

CLINTON HALL, *May* 20, 1876.

INDEX.

Early English,	1
Anglo-Norman,	1
Scotch Coins (Before the Union),	3
English Coins (After the Union),	5
English Copper Coins and Medals,	10
Miscellaneous Silver Medals,	11
Silver Coins of France,	15
Silver Coins of Spain,	17
Silver Coins of Mexico,	18
Silver Coins of Central and South America,	19
Hayti,	20
Miscellaneous Silver Coins,	20
Gold Coins,	22
United States Dollars,	23
Half Dollars,	24
Quarter Dollars,	26
Dimes,	27
Half-Dimes,	29
Three Cents,	29
Proof Sets,	30
Patterns,	30 and 90
Washington Pieces,	32
Electrotype Copies of Rare Coins,	40
Antique Coins, Greek Silver,	41
Greek Copper,	45
Celtiberia,	47
The Roman Coinage (Æs, etc.),	47
Silver Coins of Families,	48
Roman Imperial Gold,	49
Roman Imperial Silver,	50
Roman Imperial Brass,	53
Unclassified Ancient Coins (Copper),	63
Same, silver,	64
AMERICAN COLONIAL AND STATE COINS AND TOKENS.	
Massachusetts,	65
Maryland,	66
The Carolinas, Louisiana, Virginia, and New York,	67
Vermont,	68
Connecticut and New Jersey,	69
Kentucky, Rosa-Americana, and Miscellaneous,	70

MEDALS IN VARIOUS METALS—VERNON SERIES.
 Rhode Island Peace Medals,. . . . 72
 Miscellaneous, ... 73
 United States Cents, ... 83
 Half-Cents, ... 89
Foreign Medals in different Metals, ... 92
NATIONAL MEDALS IN BRONZE.
 Presidential, ... 97
 Army, ... 98
 Navy, ... 100
 Political and Presidential, . . . 101 to 111
 Army Officers, ... 111
 Patriotic and Miscellaneous, ... 112
 Silver Medalets and Tokens, . . . 114
A Cabinet of Reproductions, or Electrotype Copies from
 Originals in the British Museum, . . . 115
A Collection of Store Cards, Copperheads, etc., . 116
Numismatic History and Text-Books, . . . 116
Catalogues, ... 118
Cabinets, ... 119

ADDENDA.

Greek Coins, Gold and Silver, ... 120
Roman and Greek Imperial, Silver, ... 122
Greek, Copper, ... 123
Alexandrian and Imperial Greek, Copper, . 125–126
Roman Colonial, Copper, ... 126
Roman Imperial, Gold, ... 128
Same, Silver, ... 129
Same, Copper, ... 130
Miscellaneous.—Greek, Silver; Greek, Copper; Byzan-
 tine, Copper. 131
Phoenician, ... 133
Jewish, ... 134
Coins of Crusaders, ... 135
Modern Coins, ... 136
Antique Intaglios, ... 136

CATALOGUE OF COINS.

Early English.

1 SKEATTE of the Heptarchy. A silver coin. Obv. rude head; rev. letters and ring within square. Ruding Pl 1, No. 6.
2 STYCÆ of Eanred, King of Northumberland. (A.D. 808.)

Anglo-Norman.

3 WILLIAM I. 1066–1087 penny. Full face, with crown and sceptre. Rev. PAXS and cross. Struck at Winchester. Extremely fine.
4 —— Penny of the same type. Equally fine.
5 —— Another. Same in all respects.
6 —— Repetition of last.
7 HENRY I (or II). Penny, head crowned, sceptre to left; rev. crosses within the angles of a cross. Of rude form but exceedingly well-preserved, and very rare.
8 STEPHEN. 1135–1154. Penny, head in profile, crown and sceptre, TIFNERE; rev. cross fleurie, fleur-de-lis in angles, N : ON ; NO. Ruding Pl 1, fig. 17. Broad, in original condition, but imperfectly struck. Rare and valuable.
9 HENRY II (or III). 1154. Full-face crowned, sceptre to left; rev. double cross and three pellets in angles. Fine.
10 —— Duplicate.
11 RICHARD I. (Cœur-de-Lion). 1189–1199. His penny, struck at Aquitaine, RICARDVS around a cross; rev. PIC-TAVIE-NSIS. Extremely fine.
12 —— Duplicate. Same condition.
13 —— Another. Also fine.
14 JOHN. 1199–1216. Head in a triangle; rev. crescent and stars in a triangle. Scarce.
[See note to No. 29, Gay Collection, April 28, '75.]
15 EDWARD I. 1273–1307. Penny, Canterbury. Fine.
16 —— Penny, struck at York. Rare.
17 EDWARD II. 1307–1327. Fine penny.
18 EDWARD III. 1327–1377. Penny, struck at Bristol. Fine and scarce.
19 —— Others (Edward III. and IV.)   2 pieces

20 EDWARD III. Groat and half-groat, London. Very fine. 2 pieces
21 EDWARD IV. AND V. Groat and half-groat. (Canterbury. and Calais). 2 pieces
22 —— Other groats, different mints. 4 pieces
23 HENRY IV. 1399–1413. Gold Noble, the king in a ship; rev. cross Henric and lions under a crown, HIS-AVTEM TRANSIENS-PER-MEDIVM-ILLORVM-IBAT. Very broad and superb coin. Uncirculated.
24 HENRY VI. 1422–1461. Gold Angel, shield with arms, in a ship; rev. St. Michael. Uncirculated. Rare.
25 —— Groat and half-groat, London. 2 pieces
26 —— Same. Calais.
27 —— (or V). Fine penny.
28 HENRY VII. 1483–1509. Half-groat, profile, and numerals: HENRIC VII., etc. Fine and rare.
29 HENRY VIII. 1509–1547. Groat, style of last. Very fine.
30 —— Half-groat, same type. Fine.
31 —— Groat, ¾ face, good silver. Very fine and rare.
32 —— Half-groat, same type.
33 —— Irish groats. 2 varieties
34 EDWARD VI. 1547–1553. Crown, 1551. In almost uncirculated condition and very rare.
35 —— Half-crown to match the preceding (1551). Fine and very rare. (Plumes on the horse's head).
[These coins of Edward afford the first example of dates on English money.]
36 ELIZABETH. 1558–1602. Crown, bust in profile, with crown and sceptre, which reappear for the first time since Henry III; motto, POSVI DEVM ADIVTOREM MEVM. Not uncirculated, but fine and valuable —one of the best that have been offered for years.
37 —— Half-crown to match. Hardly as good, but more rare.
38 —— Shilling. *Mint mark*, ton. Very sharp and fine.
39 —— Same. *Mint mark*, cross with crosslets. Very fine.
40 —— Irish shilling. Base. Fine condition.
41 —— Milled sixpence. *Mint mark*, sun, 1662. Very fine and rare.
42 —— Another. Same type, 1661. Equally fine.
43 —— Sixpence, without inner circle, with loop and the remains of gilding. Well preserved. Scarce.
44 —— Shilling, sixpence, groat, threepence, twopence, penny, halfpenny, and farthing. Fine set of 8 pieces
45 —— Half shillings and twopence. Ordinary. 4 pieces

Scotch Coins before the Union.

Gold.

46 MARY. Lion. Obv. the Scotch shield crowned between the letters J. and G. MARIA D.G SCOTORVM REGINA; rev. a cypher, including all the letters of *Maria Regina*, with a star on each side and a crown above; DILIGITE JVSTITIAM, 1553. Weight, 2 dr. 18 gr. Uncirculated, and very rare.

[The letters J. and G. are explained to mean that James, Earl of Murray, was Governor when the piece was coined.]

47 JAMES VI. The King on a richly-caparisoned horse, riding with a drawn sword to right; under the horse, 1594; JACOBVS, 6, D.GR SCOTORVM; rev. the arms of Scotland crowned, SPERO. MELIORA. Weight, 2 dr. 18 gr. As fine as last. Very rare.

48 —— Duplicate of the last in all but date, which is 1599. Equally fine.

49 —— Obv. the Scotch shield crowned, JACOBVS, 6, D.G.R. SCOTORVM; rev. a sword and sceptre placed crosswise, in the upper quarter a crown, a thistle-head on each side, and below, 1601. Weight, 1 dr. 9 gr. (Half angel). Fine and very rare.

[This was the last gold coined before the union of the crowns.]

Silver.

50 DAVID II. 1329–1371. Penny. Side face crowned, with sceptre erect; rev. cross and four stars, VILLA EDINBVRGH. Well preserved and rare.

51 —— Groat. Same head, DAVID DEI GRATIA REX SCOTORVM; rev. DNS. PROTECTOR MS. & LIBERATOR MS. on a large circle, VILLA EDINBVRGH on a smaller, a cross dividing all, with four stars in the angles within the inscription. Extremely fine; rare.

52 —— Duplicate and triplicate. Good. 2 pieces
53 —— Half-groat. Same type. Pierced. Very fair.

[David the Second was the first King of Scotland that coined groats.]

54 ROBERT II. (succeeded David II.) 1371–1390. Groat, much like his predecessor's, but the legend is ROBERTVS DEI. GRA. REX SCOTTORVM (two t's). Struck at Edinburgh. Very fine; scarce.

55 ROBERT III. 1390–1406. Groat. Full face, crowned, without sceptre, legend as before; rev. same arrangement of cross and circles, but with three *balls* instead

of stars in each angle of the cross. Struck at VILLA DE PERTH. Very fine and rare.

56 ROBERT III. Duplicate. Nearly as fine.

57 JAMES V. 1513–1542. Groat. Nearly side face, and crown within a rose, JACOBVS DEI GRA REX SCOTORVM; rev. cross fleuri, with two thistle-heads and two spur-royals in the angels. Weight, 1 dr. 18 gr. In fair preservation and extremely rare.

58 —— Groat. Side face, closed crown, JACOBVS, 5, &c.; rev. the Scotch shield on a cross, circumscribed OPPIDVM EDINBVRGI. Extremely fine and rare.

59 —— Duplicate. Very fine.

60 —— Triplicate. Good.

[Groats, half-groats, pennies or halfpennies, were coined no longer in Scotland].

61 MARY, 1542–1587. A base coin with the date (1557) on both sides; obv. the Scottish shield crowned, counterstamped with a star over the letter M. to l. and R. to r.; rev. a large cross, open in the centre, in which is a small cross, crowns in the angles of the larger. Her name *alone*. Size of the half-testoon. Very fair.

[I do not find this coin described, and presume it to be rare.]

62 —— Half-Testoon, with the cypher of Francis and Mary crowned; rev. inscription in a square, JAM. NON. SVNT. DVO. SED. VNA. CARO., 1559. Very fine and rare.

63 —— Testoon. Arms of Francis and Mary on a crowned shield. to l. + to r. X :: FRAN ET MA. D.G. R.R., FRACO. SCOTORO; rev. F. and M. in a cypher crowned, supported by a fleur-de-luce and thistle crowned. VICIT LEO. DE. TRIBA. JVDA, 1560. Extremely fine and rare.

[These were all coined before her return from France.]

64 —— Base coins, minted at Edinburgh; obv. thistle crowned; rev. St. Andrew's Cross, and one of F. and M. Good lot.   3 pieces

65 —— Others of Mary alone.   2 pieces

66 JAMES VI. 1587–1625. Piece of an ounce weight; obv. Scottish arms crowned: to l. J. crowned, to r. R. crowned: JACOBVS 6. DEI. GRATIA. REX. SCO-TORVM; rev. a drawn sword upright, with a crown on its point; a hand pointing to three X's (for thirty shillings), with the date 15–67 below, circumscribed with PRO ME. SI. MEREOR IN ME. Very fine and rare crown.

[This motto was borrowed from Trajan, and suggested by George

Buchanan, the young King's tutor. This crown was the first struck by James. It will be noticed that his mother's "Yew-tree" dollar bears the same date ; also, that there is an account of several silver medals, commemorating great and sorrowful passages in the Queen's life, struck afterwards.]

67 JAMES VI. A similar piece of thirty shillings, dated 15–68, counterstamped with the Scottish thistle. Equally fine and rare.

68 —— Shield crowned : JACOBVS 6. D.G.R. SCOTO-RVM, 1591; rev. a naked sword and balance, HIS DIFFERT. REGE. TYRANNVS. Weight, 2 dwt. 14 gr. (called the *Balance Mark*.) Very fine ; rare.

69 —— Piece of thirty shillings; obv. portrait of the King's body to the waist, a crown on his head and sword in his hand; rev. arms of Scotland crowned, J. R. at the sides of the shield, and XXX—S below. HONOR REGIS. JVDICVM. DILIGIT. 1582 Nearly uncirculated and very rare.

70 —— Twenty-shilling piece of the same type, the value denoted by XX—S. Still finer than last, and equally rare.

71 —— Ten-shilling piece of this series (X—S.) Same date. Also very fine and rare.

72 —— Silver Noble or twenty-groat piece; obv. shield crowned with the figures 6——8 ; at the sides, JACOBVS, etc. ; rev. four crowned capital I's, forming a cross with crowns and thistles in alternate angles, SALVA - FACPOPVLVM-TVVM-DNE-1572. Fine and rare

[Intrinsic value same as English shilling, or nearly so.]

73 —— Billon coin of James IV. JACOBVS, etc.; rev. star of 5 points in centre of cross, VILLA DE EDINBVRG.

74 JAMES VIII. Son of James II. of England, and pretender to the crown. Silver crown ; obv. laureated bust, JACOBVS VIII DEI GRATIA ; rev. arms crowned, SCOT-ANGL. FRAN. ET EIB. REX 1716. Nearly proof. Very rare.

English Coins after the Union.

Gold.

75 CHARLES I. 1625-1649. Pound piece ; obv. crowned bust behind XX ; rev. shield crowned FLORENT-CONCORDIA REGNA. M. M. Welsh plume. Very fine. Rare.

76 —— Half pound (X S). CVLTORES—SVI DEVS PROTEGIT. Very fine and rare.

77 COMMONWEALTH. 1648–1660. Pound piece; obv. shield with the cross of St. George, THE COMMONWEALTH OF ENGLAND; rev. same shield joined to one with the Irish harp, GOD. WITH-VS, 1651, on the upper field XX. Uncirculated and brilliant. Very rare.

78 GEORGE I. 1714–1727. Coronation medal; obv. laureated bust; rev. the King seated, Britannia standing, placing a crown on his head, in ex. INAVGVRAT XX OCT. MDCCXIIII. Brilliant proof, size 22, weight 3 guineas.

79 GEORGE II. 1729–1760. Double guinea 1738, laureated bust to l.; rev. arms crowned. Uncirculated. Rare

Silver.

80 JAMES I. (James VI. of Scotland.) 1602–1625. Crown; obv. the king on horseback armed and crowned; rev. arms of the union on a shield, surmounted by the Welsh plumes. Almost uncirculated. Very rare.

81 —— Duplicate, except that on this the Welsh feathers are wanting. Fine. Very rare.

82 —— Half-crown of this type. The motto on all is QVÆ DEVS CONJVNXIT NEMO SEPARET. A fine example. More rare than the crown.

83 —— Shilling. Crowned head to r.; behind XII.; same legend and inscription. Very fine.

84 —— Another. Larger bust. Equally fine.

85 —— Shilling, sixpence, and medalet, engraved, the last pierced. 3 pieces

86 CHARLES I. 1625–1649. Crown; obv. the King in armor riding to l.; rev. arms on a garnished oval shield; m. m. rose, no date. In uncommonly fine condition. Very rare.

87 —— Same, with date (1645); on this the motto is, CHRISTO AVSPICE. Very fine and rare example.

88 —— Half crown, motto same as on 82. Fine and very rare.

89 —— Another. A variety. Good example.

90 —— Shilling; rev. shield surmounted by the Welsh plumes. Very fine.

91 —— Another; rev. RELIG: PROT, etc., in three lines, date 1643. Extra fine and rare.

92 —— Groat of this type. Fair. Very scarce.

93 —— Sixpence, pierced, but otherwise fine. Rare.

94 —— Another, with arms on a cross. Very fine.

English Coins after the Union. 7

95 CHARLES I. Two 40-shilling Scottish pieces, size of last. Ordinary. 2 pieces
96 —— Set: 4 pence, 3 pence, 2 pence, and penny, the last with the Welsh feathers within circle on rev. Very rare. A desirable set. 4 pieces
97 —— Obsidional of Newark; OBS. NEWARK, 1646; rev. a crown between C—R, below XXX; two shillings and sixpence, diamond shape, thick. Very rare.
98 —— Similar, value XII. (shilling.) Extra fine.
99 —— Similar, struck the year before; value IX. (ninepence.) Fine and very rare.
100 —— Similar, 1646, value VI. (sixpence.) Extra fine. Rare.
101 —— and James I. Rose crowned; rev. thistle crowned; 2 pennies and halfpenny. Fine. 3 pieces
102 —— Same repeated. 3 pieces
103 —— Irish farthings, rose and thistle, twopences; Portcullis farthing of Elizabeth and others. 9 pieces
104 COMMONWEALTH. 1648–1660. Crown, date 1656; V (shillings), GOD WITH VS. Almost uncirculated. A beautiful piece; in this condition very rare.
105 CROMWELL to 1660. Half-crown, 1558, PAX QVÆRI- TVR BELLO. Fine. Rare.
106 —— Shilling, proof impression, tin, milled edge. Original and extremely rare.
107 CHARLES II. 1666–1684. Shilling. Laureated bust shown nearly to the waist; struck without collar, leaving the edge rough. 1669. Fine and rare.
108 —— Sixpence. Same type.
109 —— Shilling. Milled edge. 1668. Fine.
110 —— Pattern halfpenny. Copper. CAROLVS A CAROLO; rev. QVATVOR MARIA VINDICO. Beautiful impression. Without date. Extremely rare.
111 —— Pattern farthing of this type struck in silver 1665. A little circulated. Very rare.
112 —— Twopence (silver), Bawbee for Scotland (copper), and twopence and penny of Charles I. 4 pieces
113 JAMES II. 1684–1688. Crown, 1687. Uncirculated. Rare,
114 —— Half-crown, 1686. Uncirculated.
115 —— Shilling. (10 S Scottish). Poor.
116 —— Fourpence, threepence, twopence, and penny. Maundy. Very fine. 4 pieces
117 MARY II., William and Mary, and William III. 1688– 1702. Obv. diademed head of MARIA II. DEI GRA; rev. a full-blown rose on its stem, EX CAN

DORE DECVS. Pattern farthing in silver. Extremely fine and rare.
118 MARY II. Obv. same as last; rev. head and title of William III.; also pattern farthing in silver. Circulated, but still well preserved and very rare.
119 —— Obv. laureated busts of William and Mary, with their titles; rev. Britannia seated. 1694. Pattern farthing in silver. Very fine and rare.
120 —— Half-crown. Obv. busts of William and Mary to r.; rev. cypher of their names in the angles of a cross, &c. Fine.
121 —— Half-crown. Obv. same; rev. plain shield and crown. Fair.
122 —— Sixpence and fourpence of William and Mary. The former gilt and very fine. 2 pieces
123 —— Crown of William III. 1695. Uncirculated. Rare.
124 —— Maundy set of William III. 4 pieces. Fine and rare.
125 —— Another set, all fine, but the 4d, which is fair.
126 ANNA. 1702-1714. Shilling, E under bust, and one without. Ordinary. 2 pieces
127 —— Sixpence, fourpence, piece of five shillings Scotch, &c. Ordinary. 4 pieces
128 —— Set Maundy money. Extremely fine and rare. 4 pieces
129 —— Pattern farthing, struck in silver, Britannia seated. 1713. Beautiful proof. Extremely rare.
130 GEORGE I. 1714-1727. Crown 1723, S. S. C. (South Sea Co.) A beautiful example. Very nearly uncirculated. Rare.
131 Half-crown. 1717. Roses and plumes. Nearly as fine as last.
132 —— Set of Maundy money. Very fine. 4 pieces
133 GEORGE II. 1727-1760. Crown. Obv. laureated bust in the Roman style; rev. arms on four shields arranged in the form of a cross. 1750. Edge lettered. Very fine.
134 —— Sixpence and threepence. Ordinary. 2 pieces
135 —— Set Maundy money. Fine. 4 pieces
135* GEORGE III. 1760-1820. Pattern Crown, by Mudie & Mills. Laureated bust undraped; rev. arms on four shields crossed, a crown on each shield; a rose, shamrock, and thistle in three quarters, a horse in the fourth, and St. George as a boss in the centre. Very rare and fine, with only a few slight scratches.
136 —— Bank of England Dollar. 1804. Very fine.

English Coins after the Union.

137 GEORGE III. Bank Token of 1812. Three shillings.
138 —— Half-crown of 1817. BRITANNIARVM, &c. Edge milled. Uncirculated.
138* —— Northumberland Shilling of 1763. Extremely fine and rare; only a few having been coined.
139 —— Shilling of 1787. Without dot above the head. Extremely fine and rare.
140 —— Same, with dot. The usual form. Uncirculated.
141 —— Other shillings, young and old head. Nearly uncirculated. 2 pieces
142 —— Shillings, shilling tokens, and 10d bank tokens. Generally fine. 8 pieces
143 —— Sixpences. One very fine. 2 pieces
145 —— Set Maundy money. Young head 1795. Uncirculated. 4 pieces
146 —— Another set. Equally fine. 4 pieces
147 —— Proof set of same. Old head. 1820. Rare. 4 pieces
150 —— Rupee and half-rupee of this reign. 2 pieces
151 GEORGE IV. 1820–1830. Crown, 1821. Brilliant proof from Pistrucci's dies. Very rare.
152 —— Crown from dies by same for the next year. 1822. Very fine.
153 —— Crown of 1826. Head from Chantry's design. Brilliant proof. Very rare.
154 —— Half-crown to match. Same date.
155 —— Another. Slightly circulated.
156 —— Set of Maundy money for 1829. Brilliant proof. 4 pieces
157 —— Another set. Equally fine. 4 pieces
158 WILLIAM IV. 1830–1837. Shilling, sixpence, and fourpence. Fine. 3 pieces
159 —— Rupee and half-rupee. 2 pieces
160 —— Set Maundy money; brilliant proof. 4 pieces
161 —— Another set. Same. 4 pieces
162 VICTORIA, 1837; Florin, 1489. On this the omission of D. G. in the title, caused the recall of the issue. Scarce. Fine.
163 —— Duplicate. Equally fine.
164 —— Florins of 1853. 2 pieces
165 —— Shillings. Fine.
166 —— Canada 20, 10, and 5 cents. Fine. 3 pieces
167 —— Maundy set. Uncirculated. 4 pieces
168 —— Same. Uncirculated. 4 pieces

169 VICTORIA. Another. Uncirculated. 4 pieces
170 —— Small silver, with odd coins of earlier date
amo unting to 48d., or 4s. sterling. The lot.
171 —— East Indian coins, etc. ¼ Rupees, 2 Annas, etc.
6 pieces
171* —— 50 cents and 25 cents for Canada. 1870. Uncirculated. 2 pieces

English Copper Coins.

172 JAMES II. Pewter Penny, with copper plug inserted; halfpenny size; as good as ever found. Not fine. Very rare.
173 GEORGE II. AND III. Twopenny, penny, and halfpennies. Fair. 6 pieces
174 GEORGE IV., William IV., and Victoria. Pennies, halfpennies, and farthings. Very ordinary. 62 pieces

English Medals in Bronze.

175 WILLIAM BECKFORD, ESQ. Bust nearly full face, in wig; ermine collar and sword; rev. inscription in parallel lines; Obit. 21, June 1770. Proof. Size, 26
176 ISAAC NEWTON. Bust to left; rev. FELIX COGNOSCERE CAVSAS, 1726. Proof. Size, 28
177 JAMES OGLETHROPE. Bust nearly full face; rev. bust of Archbishop Tillotson; also facing, 1737–1694. Proof. Rare. Size, 26
178 AMBROSE MERLIN. Fine medal by *Milton*, dated 1780. Merlin seated; rev. temple of music. Beautiful proof. Size, 24
179 MEDAL to commemorate the first published English Bible. Translated by *Coverdale*, October 4, 1535. Coverdale seated; rev. a Bible in chains; 3d centenary. Extra' fine and rare. Size, 24
180 WALTER SCOTT. Bust bare; rev. Muse standing. 1827. Fine proof, by *Chantrey & Stothard*. Very beautiful medal. Scarce. Size, 38
181 FREDERICK, DUKE OF YORK. Medal executed in similar style, by same. Same size.
182 WILLIAM PITT. Bust to left; rev. male figure holding rudder. By *Wyon*. Size, 30
183 LORD NELSON. His bust on a shield, supported by emblematical figure of Peace; rev. Battle of the Nile, 1798. By *Kuchler*. Proof. Rare. Size, 30

Miscellaneous Silver Medals.

MATTHEW BOULTON. In memory of his obsequies, 1809
Proof.   Size, 25
JAMES WATT. Bust; rev. steam engine. Proof.
                                                          Size, 28
ACKERMAN'S Honorary Medal. By *Pidgeon*. Beautifully executed snake ring entwined with laurel.
Proof.   Size, 26
YORK MINSTER, destroyed by an insane incendiary, 1829; the Cathedral as at present standing; rev. inscription.
Proof.   Size, 26
JOSEPH SCHOLEFIELD AND THOMAS ATWOOD. Their busts conjoined; rev. inscription. Proof.   Size, 26
VISCOUNT PERY AND FRANCIS HENRY EDGERTON. 2 pieces
SIR ISAMBERT MARC BRUNEL. View of the Thames tunnel on rev. Proof.   Size, 40
HON. EDMUND BURKE; rev. Fame. Beautiful medal.
Proof, by *Westwood*.   Size, 24
VICTORIA Coronation medal, and Viaduct over the Sankey Canal and Valley, to commemorate the opening of the Liverpool and Manchester R.R. Fine proof.
                                                          2 pieces

Miscellaneous Silver Medals.

MEDAL struck to commemorate the destruction of the Spanish armada off the British coast, in 1588. Obv. ships going down at sea; inscription: TU DEUS MAGNUS * ET * MAGNA * FACIS * TU * SOLUS * DEUS *. Within the inner circle, VENI * VIDI * VIVE *. Rev. pope, cardinal, kings, etc., " kicking against the pricks"; inscription: DURUM * EST * CONTRA * STIMULUS *CALCITRARE *, etc. Extremely fine and valuable.   Size, 32
RELIGIOUS medal. Obv. Baptism of the Saviour; rev. Scripture texts. Beautiful proof.   Size, 34
"FRIENDSHIP AND LOVE" medal. Within a snake ring, two allegorical figures flying over a globe; rev. inscription. Beautiful proof, by *Looz*.   Size, 24
BIRTH MEDAL. Inscription in German, " Unto us a Son is born. To us a Son is given."—Isai. ix.; rev. Birth of the Saviour in Bethlehem, stable, etc. Old and extremely fine.   Size, 24
RELIGIOUS. By *Looz*. FURCHTE GOTT THUE RECHT SCHEUT NIEMANO; rev. four figures standing. Fine.   Size, 24
SIGISMUND I., Emperor of Germany. 1410-1437. The Emperor crowned and in his robes, holding the sceptre

and orb; rev. relics from the manger and cross of our Lord; inscription in Latin. Struck to commemorate his gift of these relics to Nuremberg. Extremely fine. Rare. Size, 23

199 MARIA THERESE. In commemoration of her generosity to the inhabitants of Wettenhausen during a famine, in 1771. By *Konig*. View of the city, on one side; rev. citizens paying honors to her bust, etc. Extremely fine. Size, 23

200 CENTENARY Medal. Obv. sun rising over the city of Munster, 1648; rev. sun in meridian above the city of Prague in 1748. Fine accessories and fine medal. Size, 21

[The following series of ten war medals illustrate, among other great events, celebrated battles, in which Prince Eugene, of Savoy, and the Duke of Marlborough took leading parts.]

201 LEOPOLD I. Leopold in a car drawn by lions; rev. Battle of Mohaz, 1687, by W. I. H. Very fine. Size, 28.

202 —— Same. Laureated bust of Leopold; rev. another battle with the Turks, same year. Equally fine, G. H. Size, 28

203 HOCHSTET. View of the battle 1704; rev. VI SESE TERTIVS ADDAT DVX DEIS, two helmed figures kneeling; above, rays, by M. B. Very fine. Size, 30

204 MONTIS. Storming the Castle, 1703; rev. CEDVNT CAESAREIS CONFOEDERATIS, 4 crowned shields around the imperial eagle. Very fine. Size, 28

205 PRINCE EUGENE. His bust in armor, over it the chain of the Order of the Golden Fleece; rev. battle of Hochstet, 1704. Very fine and rare. Size, 24

206 PETRO VARADINUM. View of the attack, 1706; rev. Fame standing, "In memoriam," etc. Fine. Size, 26

207 DUKE OF MARLBOROUGH. His bust in armor, with the chain of the Order of St. George; rev. Mars on a battle-field, gallisacis, sevictis, Brabantia, Flandr, Et Antwerp, 1706. Very fine and rare. Size, 24

208 EUGENE AND MARLBOROUGH. Their busts, faces to face; rev. "Munimenta Occupata," DOVAY—BETHUNE, S. VENANT, ARIEN. Very fine and rare. Size, 24

209 CHARLES VI. The Emperor on horseback, 1717; rev. HAC, SVM, SECVRA. TVENTE, imperial eagle flying over the city of Prague. A little rubbed, but still fine. Size, 30

210 —— Same. Laureated bust of the Emperor; rev. battle of Moselle, 1735. Very fine. Size, 28

[End of the series of war medals referred to in last note, and beginning of a series of medals of Charles IV. of Spain.]

Miscellaneous Silver Medals. 13

211 CARLOS IV. Bust; rev. PROCLAMACION CON-
SVLADO DE MEXICO, 1789, by *Gil;* Mercury
supporting the arms of Spain. Extremely fine. Size, 28

211* —— Same. Rev. view of mines, ACLAMADU EN
LA G. DI. GUANAJUATU, etc., etc., by *Gil.*
Slightly scratched, but fine. Size, 30

212 —— Same. Rev. proclamation of the city of Orizaba,
1790, eagle supporting shield of arms, by same hand.
Equally fine. Size, 26

213 —— Same. Rev. "Jura de Sombrerete," 1791, by
same. Equally fine. Size, 27

214 —— Same. Rev. EMPERATOR INDIARVM
NOVAE CANTARIAE, 1790, by same. Size, 25

215 —— Same. Rev. PROC. EN. LA CVIDAD. DE.
VALLADOLID DE MICHOACAN. PUR SV.
ALFEREZ, R. DE JOSE BERNARDO. FON-
CERAD, 1791, three busts on a shield, two in
helmets, one bare, by same. Very fine. Size, 29

216 —— Same. Rev. SED NOS CEDAMVS AMORI, etc.,
by same. Very fine. Size, 27

[End of medals of Charles IV.]

217 LORD BALTIMORE (CÆCILIVS CALVERT.) Bust of
the Baron de Baltimore, ABSOlu. DMS-TERRÆ
MARIÆ ET AVALONIÆ; rev. bust of his Conjux,
ANNA ARVNDELIA. PVLCHERIMA. ET.
PTIMO; made by the modeler's hand and cast in fine
silver, afterwards tooled and burnished, with loop.
Original and very rare. Size, 30

218 HORAX NOCT. 1771. Three figures in the foreground,
an arm thrust out of a cloud holding the one in the
middle, which has a laureated head, behind this group a
city; rev. FIDA POLONIA GAVDET, pub ic edi-
fices, a group of kneeling and standing figures : proof
by *Oexlin.* Size, 28

219 COMMEMORATIVE MEDAL. Arbitratio Senatus Heilbronn,
1770, laureated altar surmounted by an eagle; rev.
FORTVNATOS NIMIVM SVA SI BONA NOR-
INT AGRICOLAS, man bending a bow, kine and
horses. Extremely fine. By *Pressel.* Size, 32

220 COMMEMORATIVE MEDAL. "Octava Hostandem Tributi
Vindemia, Fructus, 1748," a wine press; rev. "San-
andis Europae Vulneribus," a woman seated on a cow
lying down, Time holding two bottles of wine. By
Oexlin. Very fine. Size, 28

221 MARRIAGE medal of Bonaparte and M. Louisa. Laureated
and diademed busts of the Emperor and Empress; rev.
their nuptials. Extremely fine. By *Denon.* Size, 25

Miscellaneous Silver Medals.

222 PRIZE Medal. By *Looz*. A bee-hive, globe, artist's pallette, lyre, plough, etc., etc., on a table; rev. Time flying. Fine proof. Size, 27

223 WELLINGTON Medal. Laureated bust, "Erin Go Bragh"; rev. Harp, Edward Stevens, 1816. Very fine and rare. Size, 23

224 HARLEM Medal. "Comes Consilorum," woman seated; rev. "Arte et marte," Minerva seated. Very fine. Size, 22

225 LE BON VEILLARD. Ceres crowning the good old man. Fine. Size, 22

226 WURZBURG. Prize medal. Size, 22

227 VICTORIA War Medal. Crimea, 4 bars. Fine proof.

228 —— Same. "For the Army of the Punjaub," two clasps. Fine.

229 LOUIS PHILIPPE Prize medal. Rev. "Acteste Devouement, etc.," 1845. Fine medal, by *Barre*. Size, 24

230 SEDE VACANTE of Fulda. Crown of 1788. Fine and scarce.

231 LEOPOLD I. Crown of 1696. Very broad and fine.

232 FREDERICK WILLIAM of Prussia. Double thaler medal of 1839. Brilliant.

233 HELVETIA. Five francs of 1850. Brilliant.

234 GEORGE III. Three-shilling bank token of 1814. Brilliant proof. Rare.

235 ALEXANDER I. of Russia. Ruble of 1834. Uncirculated.

236 DOUBLE THALER MEDAL of Saxony. September 4, 1831. Busts of the King and Regent. Uncirculated.

237 DOLLAR of Maximilian, Emperor of Mexico. 1866. Very fine.

238 —— Same, with half dollar. Fine. 2 pieces

239 LIMA. Proof medal dollar of 1821. Rare.

240 GUADALAXARA. Proclamation dollar of 1822 in favor of Iturbide. Fine bust of the Emperor. Nearly proof. Rare.

241 BOLIVIA. Medal half-dollar, with bust of Bolivar, and four proclamation quarter-dollars. 5 pieces

242 MEXICO. Proclamation of 1821. Eagle on a cactus growing on a rock, surrounded by the sea. Proof Half-dollar. Rare.

243 LOUIS XVI. (France.) To commemorate his murder. "Immote par les facheux." Proof. Rare. Size, 20

244 LOUIS XVIII. Prize or honorary medal "Société de Geographie." Fine proof. Size, 22

245 MEDAL of Honor. J. G. GAHN, a metallurgist. Awarded by some society. Proof. Size, 20
246 SIMILAR Medal. S. Kilingenstierna, a mathematician. Proof. Size, 22
247 SIMILAR. J. C. Wilke. Eq Aur SECRETARIO SUO LUGENS AC-R SC STOCKH. MDCXCVII. Fine proof. Size, 22
248 SIMILAR. Carolus Will Schelle, a chemist.
249 ENGLISH Medal. " George Reigning," " Caroline Protecting," etc. Very fine. Size, 24
250 MARIE ANTOINETTE. Her bust; rev. Nemesis standing. "I 'accuse, le pege, l'extermine." Oct. 16, 1793. Fine and rare. Size, 20

Silver Coins of France.

251 LOUIS IX. 1226–1270. Denier Turnois. Obv. LVDOVICVS REX. Short cross; rev. CIVIS TVRONVS Cathedral. Rare. 2 pieces

252 LOUIS X. 1314–1316. Nearly groat size, LVDOV. Large crown; rev. divided shield, lilies to r.; large cross, with crosses in angle to l. Fine and rare.

253 FRANCIS I. 1514–1546. Bust crowned; rev. motto of France; in the angles of a cross lilies and dragons. Very fine. Size of last. Rare.

254 HENRY IV. 1589–1610. Testoon bust; rev. cross, fleurie and motto. Fine and rare.

255 —— Same. Testoon; obv. cross fleurie; rev. shield, with double coat of arms, crowned. GRATIA DEI SVM. ID. Q. SVM 1610. Very fine and rare.

256 PHILIP VI. Gros Turnois (1328). Extremely fine; scarce. Size, 17

257 —— Same. Duplicate. Equally fine.

258 LOUIS XIV. Crown. Bust, rev. cross. Struck over another coin; both impressions shown; rubbed.

259 —— Same. Bust, rev. three crowns, 1712; fine crown.

260 —— Same. Half crown, young bust, 1662. Fine; rare.

260* LOUIS XIV.; LOUIS XV.; Maria of Navarre; the Prince de Bourbon, and Louis, Duc de Vendosme. Jetons of the value of two francs each. Fine and interesting lot. 7 pieces

261 LOUIS XV. Crown of 1761. Very fine; rare.

262 —— Same. Crown and half-crown. Poor. 2 pieces

263 LOUIS XVI. Crown of 1775. Young bust. Good.

264 —— Same. Crown of 1788. Better.

265 LOUIS XVI. Quarter, eighth, and sixteenth crown, by Du Vivier. Extremely fine. 3 pieces
266 —— Same. Uncirculated crown of 1793. Old head, rev. Regne de la Loi; angel between fasces and cock. Very scarce.
267 REPUBLIC same date. Six livres, crown, rev. as last. Fine; scarce.
269 PIECES of this period of different values, amounting to six livres, or crown; the lot.
270 BONAPARTE. "Premier Consul An XI." Five francs. Uncirculated and brilliant. Rare.
271 —— Same. Duplicate, with five francs. "Napoleon, Emperor." Poor. 2 pieces
272 —— Same. Brilliant uncirculated franc of Napoleon, by *Tiolier*. 1810. Rare.
273 LOUIS XVIII. Five francs of 1815. Fair.
274 LOUIS PHILIPPE. Set of his silver coins, by *Domard*. five, two, one, half and quarter francs. Uncirculated, The five pieces sold as one lot.
275 —— Same. Five francs of 1837 and 1844. Fine. 2 pieces
276 REPUBLIC. Five francs of 1848. LIBERTE, EGALITE, FRATERNITE. Three figures standing. Uncirculated. Rare.
277 —— Same. Five francs of 1849, with head of Ceres. Nearly equal to last.
278 —— Five francs of 1848 and 1849, the same as described. Both very fine. 2 pieces
279 LOUIS NAPOLEON, President. Five francs, by Barre. 1852. Scarce. Very fine.
280 —— Same. Fifty centimes (half-franc) of same date, said to be very rare. Uncirculated. With three franc pieces of the empire. 4 pieces.
281 NAPOLEON III. Five francs by *Bouvet*. Brilliant proof. 1858. *Rare.*
282 —— Same. Two francs, franc, and twenty centimes Uncirculated. 3 pieces
283 —— Same. Set, five, two, one, half and quarter francs. Uncirculated The five as one lot.
284 VARIOUS from Louis XIX. to the Republic of '48. Intrinsic value, six and one-half francs. Poor. Ten pieces as one lot.
285 COMMUNE. 1871. Five francs struck from silver plundered from church altars; known by the mint marks, trident, A., anchor. Very fine and excessively rare.

Coins of Spain.

286 MONNERON and Pattern two sols. of 1791 and 1792. Copper and bronze. Uncirculated. 2 pieces
287 NAPOLEON II. 1816. Demi-franc. Copper proof. Rare.
288 COPPER coins and jetons from Louis XIV. Good lot. 25 pieces
289 —— Same. Poor lot. 43 pieces

Coins of Spain.

(Silver when not otherwise described.)

200 FERDINAND the Catholic and Isabella. 1474–1516. *Gold* double ducat, FERNANDVS ET HELISA-BET D, GRA, REX ET. Their busts vis-a-vis, crowned; rev. ·SVB; VINBRA: ALARVM; TVARVM; PRO; Eagle supporting shield of arms; 23¾ karats fine; weight, 108 grs. Uncirculated. Very rare.

[On this fine coin, which was struck between 1493 and 1504, the eagle of Sicily is represented with the crowned arms of Leon, Castile, Arragon, Sicily and Granada. The coins of Ferdinand and Isabella naturally have a peculiar and partial interest to Americans, although some, the late Artemas Ward among the number, have claimed that they made a great mistake when they encouraged young Colon to "go West."]

201 —— Two reals. Silver (as are all that follow); obv. FERNANDVS ELISAB. Arms crowned—G to left, 11 to right of shield; rev. REX ET REGINA CAST LEGI; yoke and sheaf of arrows. Fine and very rare.

202 —— Duplicate, pierced and rubbed, with fine pistareen of Ferdinand alone (Barcelona), having his bust crowned. Extremely rare. 2 pieces

293 PHILIP II. 1556–1598. Dollar without date; obv. coat of arms crowned; rev. arms in a tressure of arches. Rare.

294 —— Same. Dollar for Brabant, dated 1590. Rare.

295 —— Same. Pistareen of 1571, with his bust. Fine. Rare.

296 CHARLES II. 1665–1700. Dollar of 1690. Struck for Brabant. Arms on both sides. Called *Duro*, 8 reals. Extremely fine. Scarce.

297 —— Same. Half of same. Medeo duro or 4 reals. Equally fine. Rare.

298 PHILIP V. 1700–1746. 8 reals. 1731. (de Plata). Same type as 293. Extremely fine. Scarce.

299 CHARLES III. 1759–1788. 8 reals. (Pillar dollar) of 1780. Nearly uncirculated.

300 —— Same. Brilliant uncirculated dollar of 1787. Very rare.

301 CHARLES III. Quarters 3. Eighths 3. 6 pieces
302 CHARLES IV. 1788–1808. Half-dollar of 1790, and dollar of 1799. Both fine. 2 pieces
303 —— Same. Proclamation half-dollar (4 reals) of Orizaba, Mexico. 1790. Brilliant proof. Rare.
304 —— Same. Proclamation. Two reals. Quarter-dollar of Orizaba, San Louis Potosi, &c. A set of brilliant proofs. Very rare. 4 pieces
305 —— Same. Brilliant uncirculated dollar of 1796. Rare.
306 —— Same. Extremely fine dollar of 1807, and one with Chinese chop marks. 2 pieces
307 FERDINAND VII. 1814–1833. Acknowledged King in Mexico from 1808. Brilliant uncirculated dollar (Mexican) 1808. Rare.
308 —— Same. Proclamation dollar of 1808. Bust, rev. Palm tree. Proof impression, circulated. Rare.
309 —— Same. Siege Quarter of Valencia (very rare) and two others. 3 pieces
310 —— Same. Fine Silver Medal on his restoration. Struck in 1814 in Mexico. Bust. Rev. Mercury, etc. Size, 30
311 ISABELLA. 10 reals (half dollar) of 1855. Uncirculated. Scarce.
312 SIEGE and other Spanish coppers. Several rare. 10 pieces.

Silver Coins of Mexico.

313 COB MONEY. Thick type. Set of 8, 4, 2, and 1 reals. Uncommonly fine and characteristic examples. 4 pieces
314 —— Dollar. 8 reals. Very broad and nearly round. Very fine and scarce.
315 CUT Quarter Dollar, counterstamped and indented on edge. Fine and rare.
316 CUT and hammered Cob Money of 2 and 1 reals. 6 pieces
317 —— Same of 1 real. 9 pieces
318 HAMMERED two reals of Caracas. Old. 2 pieces
319 CARACAS. 2 reals. 1818–1819. 5 pieces
320 VARGAS Dollar of 1812, hammered, and as usual misstruck. Rare.
321 CROOK-NECK Dollar of 1824, from the Mint of Durango. Brilliant and uncirculated, but hardly a perfect impression. Very rare.
322 DOLLAR of the same type (*cro k-neck*) from the Mint of the City of Mexico. Same date. Very fine and rare.

QUARTER Dollars of the same type, with very broad milling. Mexican Mint. Rare. 2 pieces
—— Same. Narrow milling. 3 pieces
BRILLIANT uncirculated Dollar of 1857. Rare.
QUARTER and eighth in same condition. 2 pieces
QUARTER, and eighth, and sixteenth of Iturbide. Various types. Rare. 5 pieces
BRILLIANT uncirculated Dollar of Maximilian. 1866. Scarce.
—— Same. With half dollar (scratched.) 2 pieces
DUPLICATE Dollar. Fine.
MAXIMILIAN 10 and 5 cents. Uncirculated. Rare. 2 pieces
MEXICAN and Spanish half-reals. 10 pieces
CORONATION Medal of Augustin and Ana (Iturbide and Anna) 1823. Very fine bronze Medal by *Gordillo*. Size, 30
DOLLAR Medal of Iturbide struck in bronze. Very fine, rare.
QUARTER Reals, Mexico. 8 pieces

Silver Coins of Central and South America.

CENTRAL AMERICAN REPUBLIC 1830. Real. Same of Costa Rica 1849, and same Province de Cordova. All uncommon. 3 pieces
NEW GRANADA. "Un Peso" Dollar from Bogota Mint. 1860. Fair.
—— Same. Two and one Real. Fine. 2 pieces
COLOMBIA. Dollar of 1821. Indian head; rev. Fruit. Fair.
—— Same. Various types. 2 Reals. Fine. 3 pieces
—— Same. Reals 2, and half Reals 1. 3 pieces
PERU. Brilliant uncirculated Dollar of 1833, with counterstamp of F. T. O. and Crown. Rare.
—— Same. Dollar "Un Sol" 1864, and half Sol (dollar) to match. Very good. 2 pieces
—— Brilliant uncirculated half-dollar (4 reals), 1848.
BOLIVIA. With head of Bolivar. Three distinct types, and one without. All fine half dollars. 4 pieces
BRAZIL AND PORTUGAL. Half dollar value, pieces of 1000 and 400 reis, different dates. 3 pieces
CHILI. Two Reals and proof Medio Real. 2 pieces
QUARTER reals of Lima. 6 pieces
BRITISH COLONIAL, Mexican, etc. Intrinsic value of the lot of 6 pieces $2; as a lot.

350 PROVISIONAL Copper Coins of Spanish Guiana, under Ferd. VII. 1813. Thin pieces, with lion and castle; scarce. Various sizes. 4 pieces
351 —— Same. 4 "
352 —— Same. 4 "
353 —— Same. 6 "

Hayti and Portugese Colony in Africa.

354 PATTERN 30, 15 and 7½ Sol. for the Island of Hayti. 1808. Silver, brilliant proof; very rare. 3 pieces

355 BASE Coins of Boyer and Petion, Presidents of the Rep. of Hayti. 3 sizes. 6 pieces

356 SIX MACUTAS. Africa (about 40 cents.) Very fine.

Miscellaneous Silver Coins.

357 ITALY. Montisferat Quarter Crown of William VII., bust in cap and wig; rev. coat-of-arms. Well preserved and rare. See Madai, 4624.

358 —— Spinola. Crown of Philip I. 1640. Bust to r.; rev. A Prelate on horseback slaying a dragon. See Willenheim, 2716. Fine and rare.

359 —— A variety of small coins (Italy and Sicily), value $1; the lot.

360 —— Lucensis, St. Martin Dollar; an uncommonly fine example. 1750. Scarce.

361 —— Vigevano. Double Dollar of Theodore Trivulce. 1676. Bust in robes, collar and decorations of the Order of the Golden Fleece; rev. shield supported by caryatid figures; on the shield, a head with three faces, crowned; UNCIA MENS. See Well., 2727, where it is called rare; very fine.

[Visconti refers to Trivulce of Milan who had a famous cabinet of gems. Millin also speaks of him. The three faces on his coat-of-arms is understood to be a play upon his name.]

362 —— Malta. Thirty Tara piece (Crown) of Ferd. Hompesch, last Grand Master of the Knights of St. John. 1798. Extremely fine; rare.

363 —— Etruria. Crown of Ferdinand III. 1595. Crowned bust, with sceptre to r.; rev. arms of Florence and the Medici Family. Extremely fine; very rare.

364 —— Etruria. Crown of Cosmus II. 1619. Bust with sceptre; rev. arms of the Medici; in very fair condition and rare.

365 —— Republic of 1848. 5 Livre. Fine.

Miscellaneous Silver Coins.

ITALY. Napoleon and Victor Emanuel. Two Livre of each. 2 pieces

GERMANY. Austria, Ferdinand I. 1574. Fine Crown.

—— Same. Ferd. III. 1640; rev. city. Fine Crown.

—— Leopold, son of Charles of Steirmark. Bust to the waist, sceptre and crown; rev. coat-of-arms. Crowned 1627. Proof Crown, rare.

—— Same of 1632. Uncirculated Crown.

—— Leopold Negnon Gaeteri, D. G., Arched, Austriae, etc. 16–21; rev. same as last. (Old head); fair Crown; rare.

—— Leopold I. Emperor. Brilliant proof Crown of 1694. Ex. rare.

—— Same. Uncirculated. 1704. Rare.

—— Saxony Dollar of the eight Dukes. 1608. An uncommonly fine example, nearly uncirculated. Rare.

—— Same. John George and Augustus, and Christian II. 1610. Equally fine. Scarce.

—— Medal Dollar of 1567. "Gotha Capta." Fine and rare.

—— Thaler of John George III. (Saxony). 1689.

—— Brunswick. George William. 1657. Arms on a shield with five crests; rev. wild man. Nearly uncirculated Crown. Rare.

—— Same. Uncirculated Crown of George 1st of Enggland. 1721. Arms as a cross; rev. as last. Scarce.

—— Same. George Louis. 1706. Rev. St. Andrew. Fair Crown.

—— Same. Henry Julius. 1597. Crown known as the "Truth Dollar." See Stenz Catalogue, 2177. Fine.

—— Repetition of last; equally fine.

—— Holland Dollar of the City of Campen. Counterstamped HOL. Good for the age; rare.

—— Half Dollar of same.

—— Zeeland. Dollar of 1687. Fine.

—— Half Dollar of same, and another 1691. 2 pieces

—— Dollar of the Confederacy, milled edge, 3 Gulden (120 cents.) 1704. Very fine.

—— Henneberg two-third Dollar of 1694. A hen crowned; rev. arms crowned. Very good example; scarce.

—— Hungary. Crown of Joseph II. Emp. 1782. Fine.

—— Brabant. Francis II., 1796. Fine Crown.

—— Bavaria. Max. Jos. 1815. Fine Crown.

392 GERMANY. Netherlands. William, King 1840. Two and a half G. (Dollar.) 1840. Brilliant and uncirculated.
393 —— Prussia. William and Augusta, Thaler. 1861. Very fine.
394 —— Same. Medalet of Fred. William. 1603. One-third Dollar size. Very fine.
395 SWEDEN. Crown (I R D) of Gustavus III., 1776. Ex. fine.
396 —— Crown of Charles XIII. 1812. Very fine.
397 —— Crown of Charles XIV. 1821. Rev. 3 medallion busts (Gus. I-I Gust II. Fred.) Very fine and rare.
398 DENMARK. Crown of 1668. Frederick III. "3 Marek." Fine and scarce.
399 —— Uncirculated Coins, old and recent, one of Christian 4; worn, but rare. Intrinsic value about 60 cents. Fine lot. 7 pieces
400 SALISBURG. Splendid Episcopal Crown of 1632. Madonna and Child; rev. St. Rupert. Rare.
401 HOHENLOEH. Louis, Fred., Charles, Prince, etc. 1797. Fine Crown.
402 GENEVA. Republic. 1794. Fine Crown, head of the City; rev. Prix. DV TRAVAIL. Two ears of barley. Rare.
403 BREMEN. Helvetia, Poland, Brunswick, etc., etc.; a lot of extremely fine Coins and Medalets, av. quarter dollar size and value. Nearly all uncirculated. 12 pieces
404 MISCELLANEOUS Coins, silver and base. 60 pieces
405 RUSSIA. 5 ZLOT for Poland. Nearly one rouble. Rare.
406 —— Medalet with head of Elizabeth and statue of Peter the Great. Fine.
407 —— Miscellaneous. 10 and 5 Kopecks; 25 Lous for the Mauritius; and 24 Stivers for Ceylon. Rare. 5 pieces
408 JOSEPH II. Germany. By the City of Halle, fine Medal Thaler by Oxelin. Rare.

———

Gold Coins.

409 MEDAL of the City of Nuremberg. Quadruple Ducat, 1698, with loop. Fine and very rare.
410 DUCAT of same. Rev. St. Lawrence. 1540. Ex. fine.
411 —— Same of same. " 1617. "
412 —— Same of Cologne. No date. Ex. fine. 2 pieces
413 —— Same of Frederick (?). Emp., etc.

415 DOLLARS of Portugal, Spain, Italy, Mexico, Columbia, New Granada, and Central America. Fine lot. 14 pieces
416 SMALL gold coins of Turkey. 2 pieces
417 GUATAMALA. Small coin of Gen. Carrera. Rare.

United States Silver Coins.

Dollars.

418 1794. Good impression; fine for date, very rare.
419 1795. Flowing hair. Extremely fine, brilliant, and barely circulated.
420 1795. Fillet head. Proof *impression*. Barely circulated.
421 1796. Large inscription and date. Very fine. Scarce
422 1796. Small inscription and date. Equally fine. Scarce
423 1797. Seven stars to r, of head of Liberty. *Extremely fine.*
424 1797. Six stars before the head, etc. Very good. Scarce.
425 1798. Small eagle on the reverse. One of the finest known, and rare even in ordinary preservation.
426 1798. Large eagle and shield on rev. Very fine.
427 1799. Six stars before the face of Liberty. Very fine. Nearly uncirculated.
428 1799. Five stars to r., etc. Uncommonly fine impression. In this condition, very rare.
429 1800. Fine. But little circulated.
430 1801. Equally fine.
431 1802. Fair example. Considerably circulated.
432 1803. Fine for the date. Less circulated.
433 1804. Fine electrotype copy.
434 1836. Pattern by Gobrecht. Brilliant proof.
435 1838. Pattern also. Brilliant proof; very rare.
436 1839. Pattern. Slightly circulated; equally rare.
437 1840. Proof impression. Slight marks of circulation.
438 1841. Same in all respects.
439 1842. Same. Even finer. Brilliant.
440 1843. Very fine. Nearly uncirculated.
441 1844. Very fine. Has the proof polish, with slight scratches.
442 1845. Equally fine. Requiring the same description.
443 1846. Very fine. *Very* little circulated.
444 1847. Proof impression, with slight scratches.
445 1848. Very fine. But little circulated.
446 1849. Equally fine. Splendid impression.
447 1850. Proof. Nicked and scratched, but still very fine.

24   *United States Silver Coins.*

448. 1851. Splendid impression. One of the very few existing struck on an unpolished planchet. More rare than the proofs.
449. 1852. Extremely fine. Very rare.
450. 1853. Equally fine. Scarce.
451. 1854. Very fine. Scarce.
452. 1855. Proof impression. Slightly circulated.
453. 1856. Very fine.
454. 1857. Extremely fine. Scarce.
455. 1858. Brilliant proof. Very rare.
456. 1859. Uncirculated. Scarce.
457. 1860. Extremely fine.
458. 1861. Brilliant proof.
459. 1862. Fine proof.
460. 1863. Brilliant proof.
461. 1864. Brilliant proof.
462. 1865. Brilliant proof.
463. 1866. Brilliant proof.
464. 1867. Extremely fine.
465. 1868. Brilliant proof.
466. 1869. Brilliant proof.
467. 1870. Brilliant proof.
468. 1871. Brilliant proof.
469. 1872. Brilliant proof.

Half Dollars.

470. 1794. Very good for the date. Scarce.
471. 1795. Fair impression. Scarce.
472. 1796. Very fine and rare, one of the best known.
473. 1797. Good for date, and very rare.
474. 1801. Fine for this date. Scarce.
475. 1802. Equally good, seldom found finer.
476. 1803. Fair for the date.
477. 1805. Showing the date of 1804, from which the die was altered. Very good and scarce.
478. 1805. Very excellent impression of this date.
479. 1806. Very fine for variety. Pointed figure 6. Scarce.
480. 1806. Very good. The other or knobbed 6.
481. 1807. Extremely fine. Head to r.
482. 1807. Equally fine. Head to l. New die.
483. 1808. Nearly uncirculated.
484. 1809. Very fine.
485. 1810. Very fine. Slight marks of circulation,
486. 1811. Extremely fine.
487. 1812. Uncirculated.
488. 1813. Same.
489. 1814. Uncirculated.
490. 1815. Nearly uncirculated.
491. 1817. Equally fine. From die of 1813. Scarce.

United States Silver Coins.

1818. Fine. Shows date of previous year.
1818. Very fine. New die.
1819. Extremely fine.
1819. Equally fine. Date more spread.
1820. Very fine. Shows date of 1819.
1820. Polished planchet. New die.
1821. Same description. Slightly circulated.
1822. Fine.
1823. Very fine.
1824. Uncirculated. Scarce.
1825. Same. Splendid impression.
1826. Extremely fine.
1826. Very fine. Slightly different die.
1827. Extremely fine.
1828. Uncirculated.
1829. Uncirculated. Brilliant.
1829. Uncirculated. Polished planchet; nearly proof.
1830. Uncirculated.
1831. Same.
1831. Only fair, but rare variety. Small.
1832. Uncirculated.
1833. Same.
1834. Same.
1834. Fine and rare variety. Small date.
1835. Uncirculated.
1836. Very fine. Old type; large date.
1836. Extremely fine. New type, reeded edge. Scarce.
1837. Equally fine.
1838. Same.
1839. N. O. Mint. Old type; head of Liberty. Fine and scarce.
1839. Liberty, seated. Extremely fine. Scarce.
1840. Nearly proof. Splendid impression.
1841. Very fine.
1842. Extremely fine. Small date. Rare.
1842. Same. Large date.
1843. Same.
1844. Same.
1845. N. O. Mint. Extremely fine.
1846. Very fine. Large date.
1846. *Extremely* fine. Variety.
1847. Very good.
1848. N. O. Mint. Very fine.
1849. Very good.
1850. Proof polish. Slight marks of circulation.
1851. Extremely fine.
1852. Same. Scarce.
1853. N. O. Mint. Extremely fine.
1854. Uncirculated. Cracked die.
1855. N. O. Mint. Uncirculated.

26   *United States Silver Coins.*

	541	1856.	N. O. Mint. Same.
	542	1857.	Fine.
	543	1858.	Uncirculated.
	544	1859.	Brilliant proof. Rare.
	545	1860.	Uncirculated.
	546	1860.	Brilliant proof.
	547	1861.	N. O. Mint. Proof. Rare.
	548	1862.	Brilliant proof.
	549	1863.	Same.
	550	1864.	Same.
	551	1865.	Same.
	552	1866.	Proof.
	553	1867.	Brilliant proof.
	554	1868.	Same.
	555	1869.	Proof.
	556	1870.	Same.
	557	1871.	Extremely fine.

Quarter Dollars.

	558	1796.	Fine for date. Scarce.
	558*	1804.	Extremely fine; almost uncirculated. Very rare.
	559	1804.	Fair. One very good. 2 pieces
	560	1805.	Good examples. 2 pieces
	561	1806.	Fair and ordinary. 2 pieces
	562	1807.	Weak impression. Scarce.
	563	1815.	Uncirculated; as such, extremely rare.
	564	1818.	Uncirculated and brilliant. Rare.
	565	1819.	Extremely fine.
	566	1820.	Fine.
	567	1821.	Proof polish. Slightly marked, but extremely fine.
	568	1822.	Very fine.
	569	1823.	Fair impression. Not fine, but very rare.
	570	1824.	Good for date. Scarce.
	571	1825.	Uncirculated. Very desirable.
	572	1828.	Same. Almost proof.

[The die for the reverse of this coin shows a curious blunder of the engraver. The denomination, "25 c.," has first been cut "50 c.," and changed, the alteration showing very distinctly. The milling is also very broad.]

	572*	1828.	Brilliant proof.
	573	1831.	Very fine, and uncirculated. 2 pieces
	574	1832.	Nearly uncirculated. Proof impression.
	575	1833.	Very fine.
	576	1834.	Very fine. Proof polish.
	577	1835.	*Extremely* fine. Almost proof.
	578	1836.	Very fine.
	579	1837.	Uncirculated. Proof polish.
	580	1838.	Liberty head. Fine.
	581	1839.	Liberty seated. Very fine.

United States Silver Coins. 27

5˥	582	1839.	Very fine.
ⱴℓ	583	1840.	Very fine.
ⱴ5	584	1841.	Very fine.
/55	585	1842.	Extremely fine. Proof polish. Scarce.
40	586	1843.	Very fine.
35	587	1844.	Same.
5ℓ	588	1845.	Extremely fine.
45	589	1846.	Nearly uncirculated.
30	590	1847.	Fine. Scarce.
	~~591~~	~~1848.~~	~~Brilliant proof. Very rare.~~
/ℓ5	592	1849.	Very fine.
55	593	1850.	Very fine impression. Scarce.
ⱴ5	594	1851.	Extremely fine. Scarce.
55	595	1852.	Nearly uncirculated. 2 pieces
5ℓ	596	1853.	Without arrows. Fair impression.
/ℓℓ	597	1853.	With arrows. Proof. Very rare.
40	598	1854.	Extremely fine.
40	599	1855.	Same.
50	600	1856.	Uncirculated.
35	601	1857.	Same.
5ℓ	602	1858.	Proof. Rare.
25	603	1859.	Extremely fine.
	604	1860.	Uncirculated.
25	605	1861	Same.
	606	1862.	Extremely fine.
6ℓ	607	1863.	Proof.
ℓ	608	1864.	Same.
57	609	1865.	Same. Brilliant.
	610	1866.	Same. Brilliant.
55	611	1867.	Same. Brilliant.
4ℓ	612	1868.	Same. Brilliant.
5ℓ	613	1870.	Same. Brilliant.
50	614	1871.	Same. Brilliant.

Dimes.

3⅜	615	1796.	Very fine uncirculated impression. Broken die. Very rare.
2⅕	616	1797.	*Very* fine for date; almost uncirculated; rough surface, but desirable and very rare in this condition.
3⅞	617	1798.	13 stars. Very fine for date and variety. Rare.
25	618	1800.	Fine and rare in this condition.
25	619	1801.	Very good example.
50	620	1802.	Good example.
50	621	1803.	Large and small date. Poorer. 2 pieces
10 ℓℓ	622	1804.	Fine; in this condition *very* rare.
25	623	1805.	Uncirculated. Excessively rare.
25	625	1807.	Fair. Scarce.
25	626	1809.	Very good. Rare.
20	627	1811.	Fine. Scarce.
9ℓ	628	1814.	Very fine and sharp. Scarce.

28   *United States Silver Coins.*

629	1820.	Same. Scarce.
630	1821.	Large date. Extremely fine. Rare.
631	1822.	Very fair ; rare in this condition.
632	1823.	Very fine. Scarce.
633	1824	over "23." Fine for date and variety. Scarce.
634	1825.	Fine.
635	1827.	Extremely fine impression. Obv. proof. Rare.
636	1828.	Ordinary. Large and small date. 2 pieces
637	1829.	Nearly uncirculated.
638	1830.	Very fine.
639	1831.	Uncirculated.
640	1832.	Same.
641	1833	Extremely fine.
642	1834.	Fine.
643	1835.	Very fine.
644	1836.	Same. Scarce.
645	1837.	Liberty head. Very fine, cracked die.
646	1837.	Liberty seated. Brilliant proof. Very rare.
647	1838.	N. O. Mint. No stars. Good. Scarce.
648	1838.	Uncirculated.
649	1839.	Fine.
650	1840.	Very fine.
651	1841.	Good.
652	1842.	Very fine.
653	1843.	Extremely fine.
654	1844.	Fair. Scarce.
655	1845.	Extremely fine ; scarce in this condition.
656	1846.	Fine. Scarce.
657	1847.	Equally fine.
658	1848.	Same.
659	1849.	Splendid impression. Nearly proof. Very scarce.
660	1850.	Extremely fine.
661	1851.	Very fine.
662	1852.	Equally fine.
663	1853.	Considerably circulated. Rare without arrow heads, and one with arrows. Uncirculated. Very rare. 2 pieces
664	1854.	Very fine.
665	1855.	Equally fine.
666	1856.	Same. 2 pieces
667	1857.	Same.
668	1858.	Brilliant proof. Rare.
669	1859.	Uncirculated.
670	1860.	(San Francisco). Extremely fine. Scarce.
671	1860.	New type. Uncirculated.
672	1861.	Very fine.
673	1862.	Same.
674	1864.	Pattern struck in nickel. Extremely rare.
675	1869 and 1870.	Brilliant proofs.

United States Silver Coins.

Half Dimes.

1794.	Extremely fine. Rare.	
1795.	Small date. Very fine. Very rare.	
1795.	Larger date. Fine. Scarce.	
1796.	15 stars. Fine. Rare.	
1797.	Two varieties; one with 13 stars. Extremely fine. Very rare.	2 pieces
1797.	Two varieties (13 and 15 stars). Ordinary.	3 pieces
1800.	Fine. Rare.	
1801.	Only fair. Rare.	2 pieces
1803.	Fine, but pierced. Scarce.	
1805.	Fine. Very scarce.	
1829.	Brilliant proof. Very rare.	
1829.	Ex. fine. Proof polish.	
1830.	Equally fine.	
1831.	Brilliant proof. Very rare.	
1832.	Extremely fine.	
1835.	Equally fine.	
1834.	Brilliant proof. Very rare.	
1835.	Brilliant proof. Very rare.	
1836.	Same.	
1837.	Two varieties. Same.	2 pieces
1838.	Two varieties. One very fine.	2 pieces
1839-40-41-42.	Fine.	4 pieces
1844.	Extremely fine. Rare.	
1845.	Equally fine.	
1846.	Extremely fine and rare.	
1847-48-49.	Extremely fine.	3 pieces
1850.	Fine.	
1851-52-53.	Two varieties. Uncirculated.	4 pieces
1854.	Brilliant proof. Rare.	
18 5-56-57.	Very fine.	3 pieces
1858.	Proof. Rare.	
1859-60-61-62.	Brilliant proofs.	4 pieces
1863.	Brilliant proof. Very rare.	
1864.	Same. Scarce.	
1865.	Same. "	
1866.	Same. "	
1867-68-69.	Same.	3 pieces
Duplicates of 1859-62-63-67. Brilliant proofs.		6 pieces

Three Cents.

1851-55.	Good. Scarce.	6 pieces
1859-60-61-62.	Brilliant proofs.	4 pieces
1858.	Brilliant proof. Rare.	
1863-64-65-66.	Same.	4 pieces
1867-68-69-70.	Same.	5 pieces

Proof Sets.

717	1857.	Seven pieces.	Brilliant.	Rare.
718	1858.	Seven pieces.	Same.	"
719	1859.	Seven pieces.	Same.	Scarce.
720	1860.	Seven pieces.	Same.	
721	1861.	Seven pieces.	Same.	
722	1862.	Seven pieces.	Same.	
723	1863.	Seven pieces.	Same.	
724	1864.	Nine pieces.	Same.	
725	1865.	Nine pieces.	Same.	
726	1866.	Ten pieces.	Same.	
727	1867.	Ten pieces.	Same.	
728	1868.	Ten pieces.	Same.	
729	1869.	Ten pieces.	Same.	
730	1869.	Duplicate set.	Same.	
731	1870.	Ten pieces.	Same.	
732	1871.	Ten pieces.	Same.	
733	1872.	Ten pieces.	Same.	
734	1873.	Ten pieces.	Old style.	Rare.
735	1873.	Seven pieces.	New style.	
735*	1876.	Including the twenty-cent piece.		8 pieces
736	1864.	Small set. Cent and two cents.		
737	1865.	Same.		3 pieces
738	1866.	Same.		4 pieces
739	1867.	Same.		4 pieces
740	1868.	Same.		4 pieces
741	1869.	Same.		4 pieces
742	1870.	Same.		4 pieces
743	1871.	Same.		4 pieces
744	1872.	Same. Scarce.		4 pieces
745	1873.	Same. Rare.		4 pieces
746	1874.	Same.		3 pieces

Pattern Coins.

747 U. S. A. Bar cent. Bolens. *Uncirculated*

748 1792. "Liberty, Parent of Science," etc. Dime in copper. In fair condition. Very satisfactory example of a *very* rare pattern.

749 1792. Martha Washington head. Half dime in silver. Partly pierced (the attempt having been abandoned). Otherwise as sharp as when struck. Rare.

750 1792. Trial piece for cent. Eagle, a half shield, &c. Bright and uncirculated.

751 1803. Kettle's half and quarter eagle. Brass. Fine.
2 pieces

752 1836. Nickle two-cent piece. Proof. Rare.

753 Three-cent piece. Obv. 3; rev. III. No date. In mixed metal. Rare.

Pattern Coins. 31

"ONE CENT," within wreath. Rev. blank, silver-plated. Rare.
1851. Cent. Liberty seated. Rev. "1 Cent" within oak wreath. Copper. Plain edge.
Same. Duplicate.
Same. Thin planchet, in pure nickle, with milled edge. Rare.
1853. Cent. Obv. head of Liberty; rev. "one cent" within wreath. Rare.
1854. Cent. Head of Liberty. Copper.
1856. Half cent. Struck in nickle from the regular die. Very rare. Proof.
1856 Cent. Nickel. Adopted die. Fine proof. Rare.
1858. Set of 12 pieces. Pattern cents. *very fine lot*
1861. Eagle in copper. "God our Trust" in field.
Same. Bronze. Motto on schedule.
1861. Half dollar. Same motto in field. Copper.
Same. Motto on schedule. Same.
1862. Eagle. Copper. Motto in field.
Same. Motto on schedule.
1862. Half dollar. Silver. Motto in field.
Same. In copper.
1862. Half dollar. Silver. Motto on schedule.
Same. In copper.
1863. Eagle. Bronze. Motto in field.
Same. Motto on schedule.
1863 Half dollar. Silver. Motto in field.
Same. In copper.
1863. Same. With motto on schedule.
Same. In copper.
1863. Three cents. Head of Liberty. Rev. "3 cents," with laurels. Copper. Rare.
1863. Two cents. Head of Washington. Motto, "God and Our Country;" rev. "2 Cents" curved. Copper. Rare.
1863. Cent. Bronze. Indian head. Thin planchet. Scarce.
Same. Duplicate.
1863. Cent. Copper. Thick planchet. Rare.
1863. Postal currency. "10 cents." Aluminum.
Same. In mixed metal. Both rare.
1864. Two cents, in *nickel*. Scarce.
Same. Duplicate.
1865. Three cents. *Copper*, regular die. Scarce.
1865. Cent, in pure nickel. Rare.
1867. Five cents, by Longacre; in aluminum. Rare.
1868. Trial obv. and rev., on two planchets, from Longacre's dies. Perhaps unique.
TRIAL pieces from dies unknown; struck at the mint;

head in Phrygian cap, with stars; rev. eagle on blazing five-pointed star. Probably unique.
793 1868. Set of " 5," " III." and " I." cents, in pure nickel. Diademed head of Liberty; rev., denomination within wreath; edge plain. Rare. 3 pieces
794 1868. Set of " V.," " III." and " I." cents, nickel; different design, but similar. 3 pieces
795 1869. Same as last, except date. 3 pieces
796 1869. Set of " 50," " 25," and " 10 " cents, in " standard silver." Head of Liberty in Phrygian cap. Very rare. 3 pieces
797 1869. Same. Diademed head of Liberty. 3 pieces
798 1869. Another set. Filleted head with star on forehead. Very rare. 3 pieces

Washington Pieces.

(In copper when not otherwise stated.)

799 UNITY STATES. 1783. Very fine. 2 pieces
800 Same. Slight varieties. 4 pieces
801 WASHINGTON and Independence. Same date. Original. Very fine.
802 Same restruck. Fine proof. Silver, bronze, and copper. 3 pieces
803 Same. Varieties, with draped and military busts. From fine to ordinary. 10 pieces
804 DOUBLE-head cent. No date. Extra fine; rare.
805 Same. One fine. 2 pieces
806 CENT of 1791. Large eagle, reverse. Uncirculated. Red. Rare.
807 Same, with small eagle. Very fine. Rare.
808 HALF DOLLAR, copper. 1792. Military bust; rev. eagle displayed; head in a constellation of fifteen stars. Extremely fine. Very rare.
809 PIECE same date; rev. ins. in ten lines, " General," etc., " United States of America " on the edge. Only fair, but rare.
810 Same, but without date. Born -Virginia, Feb. 11, 1732. Rev. same; plain edge. Extremely fine. Very rare.
811 LIVERPOOL halfpenny. 1793. Military bust as before; rev. ship; lettered edge. Very fine. Scarce.
812 NORTH WALES token. Without date; rev. harp. Fair for the piece. Rare.
813 LIBERTY and Security halfpenny. 1795. Bust to r.; rev. eagle displayed on American shield; divided date, 17—95 below; lettered edge. Extremely fine. Very rare.
814 Same. Rev. Irish halfpenny. Fine.

Washington Pieces.

815 LIBERTY and SECURITY *Penny*. On edge, "Asylum for the Oppressed of all Nations." No date. Extremely fine.

816 GRATE cent. Head to r.; rev. fireplace. Fine.

817 WYON medal. 1796. Head; rev. cannon, fasces, and Caduceus in circle, circumscribed by ins. in three circles. Red and uncirculated. Size, 21

818 Same. Exact duplicate. Equally fine.

819 Same, except • legend on obverse, which has in addition to the first, "Born Feb. 11," etc. Very fine; rare.

820 Same, in tin. Fine proof.

821 TWIGG medal. Bust; rev. inscription in nine lines, "General of the American Armies, 1775; resigned the command 1783; elected President," etc. Tin. Fine proof; rare. Size, 22

822 Same. Exact duplicate. Equally fine.

823 MEDAL. Obv. bust in wig; rev. "The Hero of Freedom," etc., within wreath, with bundle of arrows and thirteen stars. Brilliant proof. Gilt. Size, 24

824 Same in bronze. Fine proof.

825 Same in copper. Fine.

826 FAME medal. Bust in Queue; rev. Fame flying over land and sea; 1803 in exergue. Extremely fine. Nearly proof, but with several small nicks. Very rare. Has been sold as high as $125. Size, 24

> Fame spread her wings and with her trumpet blew,
> "Great Washington has come; what praise is due?
> What titles shall he have?" She paused and said,
> "Not one; his name alone strikes every other dead."

827 VOLTAIRE medal. Bare bust; rev. cannon, drum, trumpet, flags, etc.; ins. in French. Fine proof, and as such *rare*. Size, 25

828 Same, on thicker planchet and in bronze of a lighter color. Extremely fine. Uncirculated and excessively rare.

829 MANLY medal. Original impression, pierced; perfectly uncirculated and very rare. Size, 30

830 Same. Restruck from original dies in light bronze. Fine proof.

831 Same. From different die, "Natus Virginia," etc., while on the other the legend is "Born," etc. By J. Manly. 1790. Fine proof in silver. Size, 31

832 Same. On extra thick bronze planchet. Fine proof; rare.

833 SEASON; or, second Presidency. Husbandman sowing seed. 1796. Copper. Very good and rare. Size, 30

Washington Pieces.

834 SUCCESS to the United States. Two sizes struck in copper. Unusually fine. Rare in this metal. Size, 16 and 12. 2 pieces

835 Same in brass. Equally fine. 2 pieces

836 MEDAL of Washington and Franklin. Their busts, without inscription; rev. beaver gnawing an oak tree; in exergue, 1776 (by R?). Proof. Size, 26

837 Same; rev., eagle flying with thunderbolts and olive branch; below, section of the world, "United States; date above. 1783. Proof. Same size.

838 Same. Duplicate. Equally fine.

839 Similar. Head of Washington alone. C. C. A. U. S. (Commander-in-Chief Army United States); rev. like last. Silver. Extremely fine and rare.

840 HALLIDAY medal (largest size.) Obv. bust, GEORGE WASHINGTON, PRESIDENT OF THE UNITED STATES; rev., fasces and sword crossed within olive wreath on draped chest, with s. s. shield on the end; COMMISSION RESIGNED, etc. 1797. Proof. This size extremely rare. Size, 34

841 Similar, reduced size (known as the Sansom medal). Extra thick planchet. Size, 29

842 Same in silver. Smaller size. Brilliant proof. Size, 26

843 Same in bronze. Fine proof.

844 Same in white metal. Fine proof.

845 PERKINS' funeral medal. Bust within wreath; rev. Urn and Young America standing on an altar; Minerva with American shield leaning on it; cannon and flags behind; "He is in Glory; the World in Tears," etc.; in ex. born and died. In tin. *Extremely* fine and rare. Size, 36

846 Same, small size; rev. urn and long inscription in two circles. Silver, pierced. Very good for piece. Size, 20

847 Same. Rev. skull and cross-bones; below, inscription in four circles pierced. Unusually fine and rare. Same size.

848 MEDAL. Bust to l. Rev. "Born Feb. 22, 1732. Died Dec. 14, 1799," within wreath; in tin, pierced. Extra fine. Rare. Size, 28

849 ECCLESTON MEDAL. Military bust circumscribed by legend ending "Inscribed to his Memory by D. ECCLESTON LANCASTER 1805;" rev. Indian standing with bow and arrow. THE LAND WAS OURS. outside of this inscription in three large circles; on

planchet of double the ordinary thickness. Fine
proof in bronze of a greenish hue. Excessively rare.
Size, 48
ECCLESTON MEDAL. Ordinary Medal and weight. Strictly
fine proof impression.
—— Same. Cast and turned in lathe, with thick and
elaborately engraved rim. Probably unique. *Certainly*
very rare. Size, 52
[A Half-penny with the head of D. Eccleston, the author of
the " Lancaster Medal," accompanies each of the two last numbers]

WASHINGTON BEFORE BOSTON. By *Du Vivier*, Paris.
Naked bust to r.; rev. group of mounted officers
in foreground viewing the embarkation of the British
Army in Boston Harbor. Fine proof. Size, 44
WESTWOOD MEDAL. Obv. bust in citizen dress; rev.
similar, but not same as 823. Splendid proof, gilt.
Size, 26
—— Same. Slight variety; heavier wreath, touching
the bundle of arrows on rev. Also, fine proof, gilt.
—— Same in bronze as 853. Fine proof.
WASHINGTON BENEVOLENT SOCIETY, 1808. Liberty
crowning Washington's bust; rev. "Benevolence,"
and in exergue NEW YORK. Long flat loop. Uncir-
culated. Almost proof impression, and in this condi-
tion very rare. Size, 27
—— Same. Loop removed. Extremely fine.
MEDAL from Series Numismatica, by Vivier, Paris. Ed-
ited by Durand. Proof. Size 26
MEDAL. Same series. Head by Bacon. Fine proof.
Same size
—— Same. Duplicate.
MEDAL by C. Wright. Bare bust; rev. inscription with-
in wreath. Proof. Size, 28
—— Same, in tin.
—— Same. Obv. bust by Wright; rev. blank. Tin,
thick planchet.
—— Same. *Extra* thick.
DECLARATION OF INDEPENDENCE. Medal by Wright.
Obv. bust; rev. scene in Independence Hall, Phila.,
July 4, 1776. Splendid proof. Very rare. Size, 58
CIVIC PROCESSION, Feb. 22, 1832. Fine proof set in
silver, copper, and tin. 3 pieces
—— Same. Copper. Fine proof.
WASHINGTON, Kosciusko, and Lafayette; their busts ac-
colated; rev. inscription divided by three oak chap-
lets. By Rogat. Fine proof. Size, 33
CRYSTAL PALACE (New York) Medal, 1853. By *Paquet*,

Phila. Bust within wreath, and chain above the head; eagle and rays; rev. view of the Crystal Palace, and ins. Fine proof. Silver. Very rare. Size, 33
870 CRYSTAL PALACE (New York) Medal, in bronze. Fine proof.
871 NATIONAL Monument Medal, July 4, 1848. Tin. Size, 25
872 WASHINGTON in centre of circle of 7 Presidents (8 Presidents' Medal). Fine. Size, 29
873 MEDAL by I. B. C. Front face; rev. eye and rays. "A man he was to all his country dear." Fine proof. Silver. Size, 24
874 —— Same, in copper and tin. 2 pieces
875 LANCASTER Agricultural Medal, by Key Awarded to Adam R. Barr, 1860. Fine proof. Silver. Size, 29
876 —— Same, in copper. Equally fine.
877 —— Same, in tin. Extra thick planchet.
878 MASONIC Medal, by Lovett, 1859. Fine proof. Size, 32
879 —— Same. Duplicate. Equally fine.
880 WASHINGTON Monument, Union Square. Obv. same as last. 1861. Same size. Fine proof.
881 FIDELI, Certa, Merces, by Lovett of Phila. 1860. Fine proof. Tin. Size, 34
882 BOLEN's Medal. Rev. "I hope that liberal allowances," etc., in eleven lines. Splendid proof by J. A. Bolen, Springfield. Size, 37
883 MEMORIAL of the Washington Cabinet, May, 1859. Fine proof. Silver and copper. Size, 14. 2 pieces
884 WASHINGTON Cabinet Medal, by Paquet. Rev. Cabinet, surmounted by bust. Silver. Fine proof. Size, 38
885 OATH OF ALLEGIANCE Medal. Silver and bronze. Size, 19. 2 pieces
886 —— Same. The set repeated. 2 pieces
887 TIME increases his fame. Fine proof. Silver. Size, 18
888 PATTERN Two-cent piece, with Washington's bust; obv. 1863; "God and our Country."
889 WASHINGTON and Jackson, by "P." Struck at the mint. Silver and silver gilt. Size, 12. 2 pieces
890 "BORN AND DIED," etc. Silver variety. Size, 12. 3 pieces
891 WASHINGTON and Lincoln. Same style. White metal. Size, 12. Rare.
892 MILITARY ACADEMY. Bust by *Paquet*; rev. Academic M r t. Fine proof. Bronze. Rare. Size, 18
893 GREAT Central Fair, Phila., 1864. Medalets in silver and copper, one pierced. Size, 12. 2 pieces

Washington Pieces.

SOLDIERS' Fair, Springfield, by Bolen. Tin. Size, 18
PAR NOBILE FRATRUM, by Wright & Bale. Washington and Lafayette vis-a-vis; rev. ins. Fine proof. Silver. Size, 18
—— Same. Duplicate.
WASHINGTON and Franklin, by *Bale*. Their heads on opposite sides. Silver and copper. Fine proofs. Size, 13. 2 pieces
—— Same; their heads full face on same side, over "Par Nobile Fratrum." Silver proof. Size, 18
—— Duplicate.
—— Artist's proof from unfinished die for same. Unique. Size, 14x18
LOVETT's (Phila.) Medals, with busts. "Born and Died." Milled edge. Fine proofs. Silver and copper. Size, 20. 2 pieces
—— Same. Thick and thin planchet. Copper. 2 pieces
—— Same. Rev. Cogan's card. Silver and copper. 2 pieces
—— Same. Duplicate of Cogan's card, in silver.
—— Same. Rev. "North Point and Fort McHenry." Silver and copper. Fine proofs. 2 pieces
—— Duplicate set. Same. Silver and copper. 2 pieces
—— Same. Rev. "Pro Patria." White metal.
—— Same, without bust (series No. 2). Siege of Boston, "'75-6," and Lovett's card. Copper and German silver. Same size. 2 pieces
—— Same, repeated, with the addition of one in brass. Thick planchet. 3 pieces
G. H. LOVETT (New York) Series "Head-quarters" at Newburg and Tappan. Copper. Size, 20. 2 pieces
—— Same. Valley Forge. Copper and tin. 2 pieces
—— Same. With head in border of shields and spears. Set in silver, with head-quarters on reverse. Rare. Size, 18. 10 pieces
—— Same. From series of "Residences." Obv. bust within wreath of roses; rev. Mount Vernon. Fine proof. Silver. Size, 22
—— Same, in tin.
—— Same. Rev. "House of Temperance." Copper and tin. Size, 26. 2 pieces
—— Same, with different reverses, copper and brass. 2 pieces
"THE FATHER OF OUR COUNTRY." Washington, at three-quarter face; rev. "Liberty and Independence,"

38 *Washington Pieces.*

Liberty seated, eagle standing. Pierced. Old and rare medal in tin. Size, 21

918 Calendar, by *True.* Silver-plated. Size, 23

919 Medals, with full-face bust on obv.; rev. "Sabbath-school Jubilee, July 4, 1842;" "He is a Freeman whom the Truth makes Free;" "The Hero of Tippecanoe," and log cabin, in copper, brass, nickel, and tin. Fine proofs. Size, 22. 6 pieces

920 —— Same, obv.; rev. blank. Thick silver planchet, and (I think) unique.

921 —— Same; rev. Harrison; rev. blank. "He is a Freeman," etc. Copper, brass, and lead. 5 pieces

922 "First in War, First in Peace," etc. Bust of Washington; "Reverse Lincoln"; bust of Lincoln and 12 stars. Fine proof. Silver. Rare. Size, 18

923 —— Same; in white metal.

[In mercy, let no man suppose the purchaser or the seller responsible for the sentiment of this medal.]

924 Bust, by *Key.* Reverses various. Copper, 2, and white metal. Size, 18. 3 pieces

925 —— Same. (Head in a cartouche); rev. "We all have our hobbies;" "Dedicated to Coin Collectors," etc.; "Edwin Forrest;" "Daniel Webster;" "Mobile Jockey Club;" "Not Transferable," etc., muled in every possible manner. Tin. No duplicates. 8 pieces

926 Bare bust. Branches of palm and olive crossed; rev. WASHINGTON on blazing sun, surrounded by circle of 13 stars. Splendid proof. Silver. Rare. Size, 20

927 —— Same; in white metal.

928 —— Bust; half length, military coat, "The Cincinnatus of America;" rev. "The Union must and shall be preserved." Silver proof. Size, 20

929 —— Same. Rev. John K. Curtis, Card., 1861.

930 —— Same. Rev. "The Union must," etc., in centre, large eye and rays. Milled edge and plain edge. Fine proof. Copper. 2 pieces

931 Bust within border of eagles and stars; rev. inscription in nine curving and straight lines. Fine proof. Copper. Size, 21

932 George Washington, President, 1789; rev. eagle displayed (similar to the cents of 1791). Fine proof. Copper. Size, 20

933 Order of United Mechanics, 1789. Token, by *R. Lovett.* "Honesty, Industry, and Sobriety." Fine proof. Scarce. Size, 16

934 Merriam's bust; rev. tomb, set in bronze, copper, and tin. Size, 20. 3 pieces

MERRIAM'S bust. Rev. Franklin; rev. Ed. Everett.
  2 pieces
—— Same. Rev. tomb; rev. Franklin. 2 pieces
HEAD. No inscription; rev. tomb, within escalloped border. Silver proof. Rare. Size, 13
HEAD and inscription; rev. Balt. Monument. Silver and copper. Size, 13. 2 pieces
—— Same. Rev. "Pater Patria," and different head.
  2 pieces
HEAD. Rev. Martha Washington. Brass. Size, 13
MERRIAM'S Head of Washington; rev. "The Hero of American Independence." In copper and tin. Size, 17. 2 pieces
—— Same as last, and another; rev. Merriam's card. Copper. 2 pieces
—— Same, and one of Lovett's Head-Quarters. 2 pieces
—— BUST, by *Bolen*. Rev. "Avoid the Extremes of Party Spirit." Thick planchet. Splendid proof.
  Size, 18
—— Same as last, with "Struck in Civic Procession," etc. 2 pieces
NORWALK MEMORIAL (Wood's series), 1869; rev. "Bought of the Norwake Indians," etc. Splendid proof. Silver by Key. Size, 24
BUST. First President; rev. Ivin's Card. Fine proof. Silver. Thick planchet. Rare. Size, 16
CARRY ME TO ATWOOD'S. Washington on horseback, rare card by Bale & Smith. Very fine and rare.
  Size, 16
WASHINGTON'S head in oval on Wolfe, Clark and Spies' card; rev. head of Jackson in oval. Brass. Very fine and rare. Size, 17
Same head. Wolfe, Spies, & Clark's (names transposed); rev. head of George IV. Very fine; rare.
Same head; rev. "New York Grand Canal, opened 1823." Fine and very rare.
"WE serve the tyrant alcohol no longer" medalet by *Bale*. Pierced, but *very* fine; rare. Silver. Size, 14
WRIGHT & BALE'S card with Washington's head on rev. In copper. Very fine; rare. Size, 12
Duplicate on thinner planchet and twice pierced.
ABRAHAM'S card, with Washington's head. Good.
  Size, 18
IDLER'S copy of half-dollar. Proof silver.
IDLER'S card, with Washington head. Copper.
Same (small) by *Lovett*. Silver; rare. Size, 13

959 Set of same. Silver, copper, brass, German silver, and tin; all fine proofs. 5 pieces
960 HEAD; rev. Robbins, Royce, & Hard's card. Represented by Wm. Leggett Bramhall. Fine proof. Silver. Size, 12
961 Set of same. In copper, brass, and nickel. 3 pieces
962 BRIMLOW'S Card; rev. Franklin; in silver, bras, and copper. Size, 15. 3 pieces
963 Same; rev. mortar; silver. Rare.
964 Same (by Lovett), small head; rev. mortar, 1864; silver. Very rare. Size, 12
965 Same, size 15, 4 varieties, brass and copper. 4 pieces
966 MINIATURE head in Wreath; rev. "I. O. U. 1 cent;" silver. Size, 12
967 Same; rev. "United Country," in oval. Silver. Size, 12
968 Same; rev. "Our Country;" silver, same size
969 Same; rev. "Mt. Holly Paper Co.," plated. Rare. Size, 13
970 Same; in copper. Thick planchet.
971 WASHINGTON Medalet, with loop, by Lovett; rev. "Our Country and Our Flag;" brass. Size, 14
972 SPIEL MARKES; fine lot. 12 pieces
973 MEDAL (overlooked) by J. H. H., bust circumscribed by inscription in 3 concentric circles. Rev. INDEPENDENCE. Eagle on shield and scroll. 1834. Tin. Size, 32

Electrotype Copies of Rare Coins.

974 SET of three (all ever made) of the second Presidency series; silver-plated. Very beautiful copies from Mr. Crosby's originals. 3 pieces
975 COPY of Wright's Washington. Size, 58
976 COPY of the Perkins Funeral medal, silver-plated. Size, 36
977 COPY of tin medal No. 973.
978 COPY of Wright's large clay medal. Size, 56
979 HALF-DOLLAR of 1792; superb copy.
980 EQUALLY fine copy of the "Naked bust" cent of same date.
981 DUPLICATE of "Naked bust," with another cent of '92. 2 pieces
982 UNIQUE Washington copper and cents of '83 and '92. 3 pieces

py of the Mob cap and Wyon Washington medals.
2 pieces
ASHINGTON and Franklin, 1783, and Twigg medal.
2 pieces
TREMELY well executed copies of two rare varieties of he " Wolfe, Spies & Clark " Card. 2 pieces
IBERTY PARENT," etc., large cent of 1792, and genuine Washington button-eye removed. Size of each 21.
2 pieces
RIOUS large and small shells, struck and electrotypes. Very interesting lot and very rare. 10 pieces
nilar lot of solid electrotypes. 8 pieces
ORE medal; very fine copy; rare. 36x26
ATTERN cents of 1792; varieties. 2 pieces
me of 1854-5. 2 pieces
GRANBY" and " Liber Natus." 2 pieces
CONFERATIO" and " Inimica Tyranny." 2 pieces
MUNIS Columbia and Aucton Plebis. 2 pieces
me, repeated. 2 pieces
GOD preserve the Carolinas." Varieties. 3 pieces
RITISH Settlement, etc.; rev. Copper Co. of N. C.
OD preserve N. E., Rosa Am. Farthing. etc., 5 pieces
ET of Pattern half-cents, viz., 1831, '36, '40 to '48 inclusive, and 1852. 12 pieces
uplicate, 1831, '36, '40, '41, '43, '44, '48. 8 pieces
LIBER-Natus," and " Colonoise Francois." 2 pieces
LIBERTY Parent," etc., and " Rosa-Ameri." Farthing.
2 pieces
ARE Franklin and " New-Yorke" Token; on the former UNITED above, and STATES below the motto, WE ARE ONE. 2 pieces
ARTHA WASHINGTON Disme and U. S. A. 2 pieces
OUNTERFEITS, copies, etc. 13 pieces
YATT's N. E. shilling and sixpence; Rosa-Americana. Farthing, Franklin Press half-penny, and Pitt Token.
5 pieces

Ancient Coins of Cities.

Greek Silver.

EGINA. Obv. a tortoise; rev. incuse of six divisions. Rare. Tetradrachm Didracum
GRIGENTUM. Obv. eagle and name of the city; rev. large crab in hollow. Fine and rare. Tetradrachm.
RADUS. Turreted head to right; rev. a standing female, ins., ARADION; in field to l. DOR—THE; all within a laurel wreath. Very good and rare. Tetradrachm.

1003 ATHENS. Head of Minerva; rev. owl, ATHE. Very fine. Tetradrachm.

1004 —— Head of Minerva, helmeted; rev. owl, a two-leaved sprig of laurel, ATHE. Fair, but struck on an oblong piece of metal. Tetradrachm.

1005 —— Rude head of Minerva; rev. a dog, ins. ATH. Very archaic and unusual; desirable. Tetradrachm.

1006 —— Obv. as before; rev. owl. Very early coinage and well preserved. Tetradrachm.

1007 BOEOTIA. Obv. buckler; rev. Diota, DARKA. Very fine and rare. Didrachm.

1008 —— Obv. as above; rev. forepart of a horse. Obolus.

1009 —— Obv. same; rev. club of Hercules. Very fine. Hemi-obulus.

1010 BRUTTIUM. Head of Victory winged; rev. Bacchus standing front face, on his head a crown, a thyrsus in his hand, in the field a rudder. Very fine and rare. Didrachm.

1011 CORINTH. Helmed head of Pallas, behind a small figure holding a Victory; rev. Pegassus. A very fine coin. Didrachm.

1012 —— Obv. Pegassus; rev. in square incusum, a helmed head of Minerva. Rare. Drachm.

1013 CORCYRA. Obv. a two-handled diota, ins. not legible; rev. the sun surrounded by rays, in a dotted border. Fine and rare. Hemi-drachm.

1014 ISTIÆ (or Histiæ.) Obv. head of a young woman crowned with vine leaves; rev. a woman sitting holding the mast and sail of a ship, ins. VIEON—ISTI. A very beautiful little coin and very rare. Drachm.

[The port of Istea is memorable as being the place where the fleets assembled before sailing to the siege of Troy.]

1015 LARISSA. Head of Medusa front face; rev. a horse and colt to r., ins. (LARI) SSION. Very good and rare type. Didrachm.

1016 —— Obv. as before; rev. a standing figure. Poor. Drachm.

1017 LEONTIUM. Head with garland of ivy; rev. lion's head in profile to right, four grains of barley surrounding, ins. LEONTINON. Very fine and rare. Tetradrachm.

[It was a pardonable fiction of the Leontians that these grains of barley typified the fertility of their soil. The Ancients had ever some d-vice to disclose the truth to the initiated and conceal it from the vulgar. Now that the veil of Isis has been lifted, and the mysteries of Ceres exposed to the light of day, it is not surprising that the practical modern mind should see in this reverse the simple story that John Barleycorn makes his votaries as bold as a lion. A friend adds the suggestion that this view finds support in the ancient proverb, "Leontini semper ad pocula."]

Ancient Coins of Cities. 43

1018 MALEA. Peloponessus. Obv. a large M occupying the field of the coin, below a caduceus; rev. a bird flying to left. Very rare and fine. Drachm.

1019 MESSANA (Sicily). Obv. biga drawn by mules; rev. MESENION, hare running. Extremely fine. Tetradrachm.

[This city was the ancient ZANCLE; it took this name 492 B.C., after its capture by Anaxilaos, tyrant of Rhegium. The coins of Messana are therefore very old.]

1020 METAPONTUM. Head of Ceres to l.; rev. ear of wheat, META. Very good. Didrachm.

1021 Same. Didrachm, head to r. Extremely fine.

1022 NEAPOLIS. Head of Diana to l. behind owl; rev. a flying Victory crowning the Minotaur NEAPOLITON. Fine and rare. Didrachm.

1023 PERGAMOS. Serpent issuing from the mystic chest; rev. two serpents entwined. Rare; good. Tetradrachm.

1024 RHODES. Head in profile to r., crown of rays; rev. a rose in incusum. Very fine and rare. Drachm.

1025 Same. Full face, head of the sun; rev. a rose INETOR. Fine. Drachm.

1026 SYRACUSE; head of Venus to left; rev. a bull, ins. above, SYRAKOSION; very fine, hemi-stater. GOLD.

1027 —— Head of Arethusa, four dolphins surrounding, ins. as before; rev. Biga and flying Victory. Very fine and desirable. Tetradrachm.

1028 SIDE; helmed head of Minerva to r.; rev. a winged Victory, with wreath in hand, double-headed axe in field, ins. KLEY. Fine and rare. Tetradrachm.

1029 THASUS; young head of Bacchus, crowned with vine leaves and fruit; rev. Hercules standing, resting on a club, ins. ERAKLEOY, SOTEROS, THASIONS. Very fine and rare. Tetradrachm.

1030 THURIUM; head of Mineron helmed; rev. a bull to r.; in ex. a fish, ins. THOYRION. Extremely fine. Didrachm.

1031 —— Obv. and rev. same as above. Hemidrachm.

1032 TARENTUM; obv. a horseman; rev. Taras on a dolphin holding a small Victory in right hand. Very good and rare. Didrachm.

1033 Same, duplicate. Very fine. Didrachm.

1034 Same; female head to l.; rev. a horseman; behind a star; a dolphin under the horse. Very fine and rare type. Didrachm.

1035 TYRE (Phœnicia); laureated head of Hercules (?) to r.; rev. Eagle on rudder; club palm and date in field. Very fine. Tetradrachm.

1036 VELIA; head of Minerva scyllæ on helmet; rev. a lion devouring his prey. Very fine. Didrachm.

1037 UNKNOWN, two coins in poor condition. 2 pieces

1038 PHILIP II. 359-366 B.C.; head of Jupiter laureated and bearded; rev. Quadriga of elephants, an•anchor in field. In fair preservation and very rare type. Tet.

1039 ALEXANDER III. (Magnus) 366 to 324 B.C. Head of Hercules, with lion's skin head-dress; rev. seated figure of Jupiter holding a bird in right hand, ins. ALEX-ANDROU; obv. Very fine. Tetradrachm.

1040 —— Head as before, paws knotted under the chin; rev. as above, wreath in field, DI under the chair; ins. ALEXANDROU, BASILEON. A perfect and beautiful specimen. Rare. Tetradrachm.

1041 —— Obv. similar to the above, but struck on one side of the planchet; rev. seated Jupiter, ins. ALEXANDROU. But little worn. Tetradrachm.

1042 —— Obv. and rev. as before, but a finer coin. Tetradrachm.

1043 —— Another fine specimen; obv. in very high relief. Preservation remarkable. Tetradrachm.

1044 —— As above, both obv. and rev. in splendid preservation. Tetradrachm.

1045 —— As before, but preservation not as good. Tetradrachm.

1046 —— Same description as above. Fair examples. Tetradrachms. 2 pieces

1047 —— As above. Preservation very good. Tetradrachms. 2 pieces

1048 —— Two of the usual type, one good, one pierced. Drachms. 2 pieces

1049 —— Obv. helmed head of Minerva; rev. Victory extending a wreath. Rubbed. Drachm.

1050 PHILIP III. (Aridœus, half-brother of Alexander). Exact type of Alexander's coins, except the inscription. On this, a radiated head, front-face, in the field, makes it a remarkable coin. Extremely fine. Tetradrachm.

1051 LYSIMACHUS, 324 to 292, B.C.; head of the King diademed, and wearing the horn of Ammon; rev. Minerva seated, holding a small Victory in right hand, ins. BASILEOS, LYSIMAXOY. A noble, well-spread coin. Tetradrachm.

1052 Same. Broad and well preserved. Tetradrachm.

1053 Same. Indent under chain. Fine drachm.

Ancient Coins of Cities. 45

1054 PTOLEMY I. (Soter.) B.C. 285. Fine, expressive head of the King to right; rev. Eagle standing on a thunderbolt, ins. PTOLEMAIOU. Very fine and rare. Tetradrachm.

1055 DEMETRIUS I. (Soter.) 163 to 161, B.C.; head to r., diademed, within border; rev. female seated, cornucopia in left hand, ins. BASILEOS, DEMETRIOY; in ex. II. Good and rare. Tetradrachm.

1056 HIERO II. (Syracuse); head of Ceres; rev. Cavalier. Good and very rare. Didrachm.

1057 ANTIOCHUS IV. 176 to 163 B.C.; diademed head to right; rev. seated figure of Jupiter, ins. BASILEOS, ANTIOXOY, THEOY, EPIPHANOY, NIKII OPOY. A remarkably fine coin. Tetradrachm.

1058 Same. Drachm. Same type. Beautiful.

1059 ANTIOCHUS VIII. (Grypus.) 124 to 96 B. C. Head of the King diademed to right; rev. within a wreath a seated figure of Jupiter holding a Victory, ins. BASILEOS, ANTIOXOY, EPIPHANOY. Extremely fine and rare. Tetradrachm.

1060 —— A duplicate. Equally fine and beautiful; rare. Tetradrachm.

1061 PHILIP (Philadelphus). 95 B. C. Head to right; rev. a seated Jupiter holding a spear and Victory; rev. titles in four lines of stippled letters. Much rubbed on both sides and base, but rare. Tetradrachm.

1062 ANTIOCHUS IX. (Philopater). 111 B. C. Bearded head of the King; rev. standing figure of Minerva holding a Victory, ins. BASILEOS, ANTIOXOY, PHILOPATEROS. In fine preservation; doubtful. Tetradrachm.

1063 ARSACES (which King uncertain). Head to left, fully bearded and helmeted; rev. seated figure holding a bow, a double row of stippled letters surrounding. Very fair and rare. Drachm.

1064 Same. Another type, and perhaps King. Fine. Drachm.

1065 Same XXI. (Gotafes). Draped bust; rev. figures seated and standing. Fine and rare. Tetradrachm.

Copper.

1066 ATHENS. Head of Minerva; rev. owl. Small.
3 pieces

1067 AGATHOCLES. Obv. female head, SOTEIRA; rev. thunderbolt.

1068 —— Obv. head of the tyrant; rev. winged thunderbolt.

1069 CARTHAGE female head; rev. horse standing and palm tree, and one other. Both very fine. 2 pieces

1069a BRUTTIUM. Helmeted head of Mars; rev. female figure with spear and shield, ins. BRUTTIUM. One fine. Size, 17. 2 pieces

1069b —— Obv. head to right; rev. a flying bird, ins. BRET—TIUM. Fair. Size, 12

1069c CHIOS. Obv. bearded head; rev. a diota, a wreath surrounding. A good coin. Size, 13

1069d HERO II. Syracuse. Obv. head to left; rev. a horseman. Size, 16

1070 MAMERTINI. 300 B.C. Obv. fine head of Jupiter; rev. a warrior charging. Fair. Size, 16

1071 POSIDONIA and Amphipolis. Colonial coins. Size, 12. 2 pieces

1072 SICILY. Obv. head; a figure standing holding a horse. Poor. Size, 16. 2 pieces

1073 THESSALY. Obv. female head; rev. a warrior holding a shield and about to cast a spear, ins. THESSALON. Very good. Size, 12

1074 —— Obv. head of Jupiter laureate; rev. as before. Fair. Size, 10

1075 THURIUM. Obv. head to left; rev. a bull. Fair. Size, 14

1076 A lot of seven coins, various. Poor. 7 pieces

1077 DARDANUS. Obv. head and bust to right; rev. a serpent with head erect and about to spring, ins. DARD. A curious and well-preserved coin, in shape and form similar to the large brass of the Ptolemies. *Very* rare. Size, 20

1078 LARISSA. Obv. head of Medusa; rev. helmed head of Minerva, ins. AMKAR. Rare and valuable. Size, 16

1079 BRUTTIUM. Obv. helmed head of Mars; rev. a Victory crowning a trophy of arms. Poor, but rare type. Size, 16

1080 A lot of three coins, one villon of Sidon. Poor. 3 pieces

1081 PTOLEMY. Obv. head of Jupiter; rev. an eagle standing. One of the ponderous brass of that period. Poor. Size, 25

1082 —— Another specimen, but smaller. Size, 22

1083 —— As above. Very poor. Size, 18

The Roman Coinage.

Ancient Copper Coins of Spain.

(*Celtiberia.*)

[The coins that follow in the next few lots form a most interesting and desirable series, which will amply repay the numismatic student for his labor in deciphering. Here may be found coins of the ancient cities of Gades, Bactica, Barsaba, Iliberis, etc., and he is recommended to the publications of M. De Saulcy, H. Noel Humphreys, and other learned authors for further information, as the limits of a catalogue prepared for a public auction will not allow a more extended description.]

1084	COINS OF SPAIN.	Average size, 14.			10 pieces
1085	——	"	"	"	10 pieces
1086	——	"	"	"	10 pieces
1087	——	"	"	"	10 pieces
1088	——	"	"	"	10 pieces
1089	——	"	"	"	10 pieces
1090	——	"	"	"	10 pieces
1091	——	"	"	"	10 pieces
1092	——	"	"	"	10 pieces
1093	——	"	"	"	13 pieces

The Roman Coinage.

Divisions of the Æs Libralis.

1094 ÆS. Head of Janus, bifrontal; rev. prow of a ship, ins. in ex. ROMA. Fair. Size, 20

1095 SEXTANS. Head of Mercury; rev. prow. Fine. Size, 19

1096 SEXTANS. Head of Mercury; rev. prow. Fine. Size, 17

1097 UNCIA. Head of Mercury; rev. prow. Rev. very fine. Size, 12

1098 AES; head of Jupiter to right; rev. prow. Fair. Size, 17

1099 UNCIA; head of Minerva to left; rev. prow, ins. ROMA. Very fine. Size, 16

1100 TRIENS; head of Minerva helmeted; rev. prow, ins. ROMA. Fair. Size, 15

1101 TRIENS; head of Minerva; rev. prow. Fair. Size, 13

1102 TWO specimens; value not visible. Poor. Size, 15. 2 pieces

1103 THREE parts of the Aes, struck by some of the Roman families. One very fine. Size, 12. 3 pieces

1104 PARIS of the Aes. Some fine. 9 pieces

Silver Coins of Roman Families.

1105 AEMILIA; veiled head of Vesta; PAVLVS, LEPIDVS, CONCORDIA; rev. a trophy; Lepidus and Perseus on each side, TER PAVLLVS. Very fine and scarce.
1106 ——— A duplicate, also very fine.
1106* ANTESTIA; head of Rome; rev. the Dioscuri, mounted; in ex. ROMA. Good.
1107 ——— A duplicate; rev. a chariot drawn by two stags; in ex. ROMA; and one other, brass. 2 pieces
1108 ANTONIA; galley IIIVIR; rev. standards, XIII. Poor.
1109 AQUILLIA; head, VIRTVS; rev. SICIL, M. AQUIL. Poor.
1110 CASSIA; veiled head of a vestal virgin behind a lamp; rev. figure sacrificing, LONGIN, III, VIR. Good.
1111 CALPURNIA; head of Mercury; rev. biga. Good.
1112 ——— Female head; rev. biga of stags; grasshopper underneath, CAL. Very fine and sharp.
1113 CARVILLIA; head of Rome; rev. quadriga. Good. 2 pieces
1114 CAECILIA; bearded head, PIUS; rev. an elephant; SCIPIO IMP. Fine and rare.
1114* CLAUDIA; female head; rev. a figure holding two standards; P. CLODIVS; two pieces; and one other. 3 pieces.
1115 CLOULIA; head; rev. Victory crowning a trophy, T. CLOV. Scarce, good. Quinarius.
1116 EGNATULEIA; head, C. EGNATVLE, C.F.; rev. Victory crowning a trophy, ROMA. Very good and scarce. Quinarius. 2 pieces
1117 FLAMINIA; head of Rome, ROMA; rev. Victory in a biga, L. FLAM, in ex. CILO. Very good. 2 pieces
1118 FLAVIA; head of Rome; rev. a biga; and one other. Good. 3 pieces
1119 FVRIA; head of Ianus bifrons, FVRI; rev. Victory and trophy, ROMA. Poor.
1120 HOSIDIA; female head, GETA; rev. a boar and dog, in ex. C. HOSIDI. Very good and rare.
1121 JULIA; winged female head, behind a trident; rev. quadriga, XVIIII, in ex. L. IVLI. BVRSO. One very fine. 2 pieces
1122 ——— Female head; rev. Aeneas carrying his father; CAESAR. Fair, and very rare type.
1123 MARCIA; head of Rome; rev. a biga, two standards under the horses, MARC-ROMA. Good.

[EMMIA ; a laureated head ; rev. the Dioscuri standing beside their horses, MEMMI. Very fine and well spread coin, rare.
'ORCIA ; head of Rome; rev. biga, C. CATO. Fair.
—— Head of Rome ; rev. quadriga, M. POR. Good.
2 pieces
'OSTUMIA ; head of Diana, with bow and quiver ; rev. a priest standing before an altar, about to sacrifice a bull, A. POST. A. F. Fine and rare.
{UBRIA ; head, DOSSEN ; rev. Victory before an altar, ins. L. RVBRI. One very fine, rare. 2 pieces
'HORIA ; head with goat-skin hood, L. S. M. R.; rev. a bull bounding to right above the letter D, ins. L. THORVS-BALBVS. Very fine and rare type.
'ITIA ; female head ; rev. Pegasus rearing on a pedestal, which is lettered Q. TITI. Fine and rare reverse.
'IBIA ; female head laureate, PANSA ; rev. quadriga, C. VIBIVS. Good. 2 pieces
'ARIOUS types, in poor condition. 4 pieces
—— types of the Quinarius. Some fine. 7 pieces
—— " " " Poor. 7 pieces
!OMAN sestertius ; head of Rome; rev. quadriga. Fair and very rare, seldom appearing at our sales.
2 pieces

Roman Imperial Coins.

Gold.

.UGUSTUS; laureated head to right, CAESAR, AVGVSTVS, DIVI PATER, PATRIAE ; rev. two figures standing with shields between, sacrificial instruments above, ins. surrounding, in ex. C. CAESAR. Very valuable and interesting coin, being a restoration by Caligula. *Very fine, weight about 5.00*
IBERIUS ; laureated head to right, TI. CAESAR DIVI, AVG, F. AVGVSTVS ; rev. seated figure 1olding a spear and olive branch, PONTIF, MAXIM. Very fine and rare.
OMITIAN ; head to right laureate, CAESAR. AVG, ?. DOMITIANVS ; rev. figure *kneeling on right knee* naking an offering of a standard which he holds in 1is right hand, COS. V. Very fine and rare.
ERVA ; head to right and laureated, IMP, NERVA, JAES, AVG, P, M, T, R, POT. II ; rev. sacrificial nstruments, PATER, PATRIAE. Very fine and are.

1140 TRAJAN; head to right, aos befre, DIVO TRIANO, PARTH, AVG PATRI; rev. a peacock, no ins. Very fine and rare type.

1141 HADRIAN; bearded head to left, HADRIANVS, AVG, COS. III, PP.; rev. a reclining figure holding in right hand a branch of olive, HISPANIA. Highly preserved and very rare type.

1142 ANTONINUS; head to right and laureate, ANTO-NINVS, AVG, PIVS, P. P. I. M. P. II; rev. Victory marching to left, a wreath in right hand, POT, X, COS IIII. An extremely beautiful specimen and rare.

1143 —— As above, and same ins.; rev. the Emperor holding a ball in his right hand, T. R. POT, XIX, COS IIII. Extremely fine and rare.

1144 —— As before; rev. a standing figure, a hasta in right hand and cornucopia in left, GENIVS, POP, ROMANI. Very fine and rare.

1145 MARCUS AURELIUS; head and bust to right, AVRELIVS, CAESAR, AVG, PII, FIL; rev. the Emperor standing holding a Victory in right hand, TR, POT, VIIII, COS II. Very beautiful and pleasing coin.

1146 —— Head and ins. as before; rev. Ceres standing with offerings in both hands, TR, POT, II, COS II. Very beautiful, even finer than the preceding, very rare.

1147 JUSTINIANUS; bust, full face and helmeted, D. N. IVSTINIANVS, P. F. AVG; rev. a Victory, a sceptre and mund, in ex. CONOB. Brilliant and rare *but not very*

1148 CONSTANTINE; bust, front face, holding a mund, CONSTANTINVS, P. P. AVG; rev. a base of four steps surmounted by a double cross, VICTORIA, AVG. Brilliant and rare.

1148a ~~UNKNOWN~~; obv. head to right; rev. a Pegasus, his legs being made up of a series of dots, curious size, about half aureus. Very good. *but somewhat rubbed This is An Early British Gold Coin* Silver.

1148b AUGUSTUS; head of Augustus; rev. Victory standing on a chest, serpent on each side. Fine, and one other rare. Quinarii. 2 pieces

1149 CLAUDIUS; head of the King, CLAVD. CAESAR; rev. Victory inscribing a shield, her right foot on a ball. Good and rare. Quinarius.

1150 VESPASIAN, A.D. 69; head of Vespasian; reverses different. Fair. 2 pieces

1151 —— As above. Fair. 2 pieces

1152 TITUS, A.D. 79; head, IMP. TITVS, CAESAR,

Roman Imperial Coins. 51

    VESPASIAN, AVG ; rev. a temple, T. R. P. IX, etc. Fair.
153 DOMITIAN, A.D. 81 ; head, IMP. CAES. DOMIT. AVG ; rev. Victory with shield and spear, long ins. surrounding. Very fine and sharp.
154 —— Head and ins.; rev. Minerva standing, holding a spear. Very fine.
155 —— Same; rev. Pegasus standing. Fine.
156 —— Same; different reverses. Good.   2 pieces
157 —— " " " "   2 pieces
158 —— " " " "   2 pieces
159 —— " " " "   2 pieces
160 —— " rev. a cistophorus. Poor but rare. Quinarius.
161 TRAJAN, A.D. 98 ; head, IMP, CAESAR, TRAI- ANO, AVG, GER.; rev. seated figure of the King, ins· surrounding. Good.   2 pieces
162 —— Same; different reverses. Good.   4 pieces
163 —— " " " "   6 pieces
164 —— " " " Some good.   7 pieces
165 HADRIAN, A.D. 117; head, HADRIANVS' AVGVSTVS ; Fortune standing, and two others· Good.   3 pieces
166 —— Same; reverses various. Good.   3 pieces
167 —— " " " "   4 pieces
168 —— " " " Fair.   4 pieces
169 SABINA (wife of Hadrian) ; head with title and ins.; rev. standing figure, PVDICITIA. Fair.
170 ANTONINUS PIUS, A.D. 138 ; head bearded and laureate, ANTONINVS AVG, PIVS. ; different re- verses. Sharp and bright as when minted. Extreme- ly fine.   5 pieces
171 —— As above, all extremely fine.   5 pieces
172 —— " " "   5 pieces
173 —— " " "   5 pieces
174 —— " " "   10 pieces
175 —— " " "   10 pieces
176 —— " " "   10 pieces
177 —— " " "   10 pieces
178 —— " " "   10 pieces
179 —— " " "   10 pieces
180 —— " " "   10 pieces
181 —— " " "   12 pieces

1182 FAUSTINA (the elder); head of Faustina, hair plaited and arranged with a small corona on top. and partly *veiled;* DIVA FAVSTINA ; rev. the Empress standing, AETERNITAS. Very fine and scarce type.
1183 —— As above, but the heads not veiled, reverses, a standing figure. Extremely fine. 4 pieces
1184 —— As above, all extremely fine. 4 pieces
1185 —— " " " 4 pieces
1186 —— " " " 4 pieces
1187 —— " " " 4 pieces
1188 —— " " " 4 pieces
1189 —— " " " 4 pieces
1190 MARCUS AURELIUS, A.D. 161; bearded head of the King.' IMP. M. ANTONINVS. AVG.; reverses various. All extremely fine and uncirculated. 5 pieces
1191 —— Uncirculated and extremely fine. 5 pieces
1192 —— " " " 5 pieces
1193 —— " " " 4 pieces
1194 FAUSTINA (the younger); head, FAVSTINA. AVGVSTA. Different reverses. Very fine. 4 pieces
1195 —— As above, all fine. 4 pieces
1196 —— " all good. 5 pieces
1197 LUCIUS, VERUS. A.D. 161. (Associated with M. Aurelius); head, IMP. L. AVREL. VERVS. AVG; rev. standing figure. Extremely fine and sharp. 2 pieces
1198 —— As above, extremely fine and sharp. 3 pieces
1199 —— " " " 3 pieces
1200 LUCILLA (wife of Verus); head, LVCILLAE, AVG, ANTONINVS; rev. CONCORDIA. Fair and *rare.*
1201 PERTINAX; head bearded and laureate. CAES. P. HELV. PERTIN. AVG; rev. Justice standing, ins. surrounding. Fair and very rare.
1202 SEPTIMUS SEVERUS, A.D. 198. Head laureate; rev. Victory standing, VICTORIA, AVG. Uncirculated and beautiful.
1203 —— As above, extremely fine, but dark color. 2 pieces
1204 CARACALLA, A.D. 211. Head; rev. female figure. PMTRF. XVII., etc. A beautiful coin, as it came from the dies. Rare.
1205 —— A duplicate; obv. very fine.
1205*—— As above, very good. 2 pieces
1206 GETA, (brother of Caracalla); head; rev. a figure standing beside a trophy. PRINC. IVVENTATIS. Very good and rare, but pierced.
1207 ELAGABALUS, A.D. 218. Head; rev. FIDES MILITVM. Very fine and large coin, rare. Size, 14

Roman Imperial Coins. 53

1208 ELAGABALUS, A.D. 218; rev. a galley. FELICI-
TAS TEMP, and one other, fine. 2 pieces

1209 JULIA SOEMIAS, (mother of Elagabalus); head; rev.
female figure. VENVS CAELESTIS. Very fine
and scarce.

1210 —— Same; rev. Venus standing. Equally fine, scarce.

1211 JULIA MAESA. Head; rev. a sitting figure.
PVDICITIA. Fair.

1212 SEVERUS ALEXANDER, A.D. 222; head; rev.
standing figure, ANNON AVG. Extremely fine;
bright and sharp. Scarce.

1213 JULIA MAMAEA (mother of Sev. Alex.); head; rev.
standing figure, IVNO CONSERVATRIX. Fine.

1214 MAXIMINUS I; head laureate; rev. soldier between
two standards, FIDES MILITVM. Fine.

1215 OTACILIA SEVERA (wife of Philip I.); head; rev.
seated figure, CONCORDIA AVGG. Very fine.
Size, 15

1216 —— Head, as above; rev. a hippopotamus, SAECVL-
ARES AVGG. Good and rare reverse.

1217 ETRUSCILLA (wife of Decius); head; rev. standing
figure, PVDICITIA. Very fine.

1218 POSTUMUS, A.D. 267; head, with open pointed
crown; rev. standing figure, SALVS POSTVMI
AVG. Very fine, and one other. 2 pieces

1219 JULIAN II. (the Apostate), A.D. 363; head, banded,
IVLIANVS PFHV; rev. in a wreath, VOTIS,
MVLTIS, X. Very fine.

1220 CONSTANTINE (uncertain); head, D.N. CONSTAN;
rev. a wreath, VOTIS XXX MVLTI, XXXX. Fine.

Brass.

1221 SEXTUS POMPEY, B.C. 49; head of Ianus, bifrontal;
rev. prow of a ship. Poor, but rare. 2 sizes.
2 pieces

1222 AUGUSTUS, B.C. 31; rude head to right; rev. a non-
descript animal; a colonial coin struck probably in
Spain. Poor, but interesting. G. B.

1223 —— Head laureate, DIVOS JVLIVS; rev. head of
Augustus DIVI, F. CAESAR; perfectly patinated,
in very fair preservation. Rare. G. B.

1224 —— A duplicate; condition not quite as good. Rare.
G. B.

1225 —— Three varieties. Fair. M. B. 3 pieces
1226 —— Two " " M. B. 2 pieces

1227 AUGUSTUS, B.C. 31. Laureated head to left. DIVVS. AVGVSTVS, PATER; rev. Rome seated holding a spear, S. C. Very fine and valuable, perfectly patinated. M. B.

1228 —— As above; reverses different. Good. M. B. 2 pieces

1229 —— " " " " Fair. M. B. 2 pieces

1230 —— Heads of Augustus and Agrippa, IMP. DIVI. F.; rev. a crocodile chained to a palm-tree, CUL-NEM. A beautiful coin, perfectly patinated, very desirable. M. B.

1231 —— A duplicate; obv. very fine, patination perfect. M. B

1232 —— Duplicate; fine green patination, everything legible. M. B.

1233 —— Duplicates. Poor. M. B. 3 pieces

1234 JULIA AVGUSTA (wife of Augustus); fine head to right, SALVS AVGVSTA; rev. a long ins. surrounding, S. C. in field. Very good and rare. M. B.

[Of the coins of this Princess struck in Rome, there are three types, and she is represented on them as Piety, Justice, and Health.]

1235 AGRIPPA (son-in-law of Augustus); laureated head to left, M. AGRIPPA, F. COS III.; rev. Neptune standing holding a trident, S. C. Very fine. M. B.

1236 —— As before, duplicates. Very good. M. B. 2 pieces

1239 TIBERIUS, A.D. 14; head to the left, ins. (TI) CÆSAR, DIVI, AVG, PRON. AVG, F. M. TRP III.; rev. a wreath of oak leaves encircling the ins., S. P. Q. R.—P. P.—OB, CIVES—SERVATOS. Very good, and excessively rare. G. B.

[Particular attention is called to the above rare coin. It will be noticed that the first letters, TI, have been broken ˚off, and the damaged part is filled with a green patination. The head has been injured by a severe blow, somewhat defacing it. Numismatic authors say that after the death o Tiberius his coins were called in and destroyed, in execration of the tyrant.]

1240 TIBERIUS; head laureate to the left, ins. TI CÆSAR, DIVI, AVG, etc.; rev. a caduceus between two cornucopiæ, PONT, MAX, COS, etc A very fine and satisfactory coin; fine black patination; very rare. M. B.

1241 —— Two varieties, heads right and left; reverses different. Very good. M. B. 2 pieces

1242 —— Head to right, TI. AVG; two horses. Rather poor, but scarce. S. B.

1243 GERMANICUS; head to left; rev. inscription sur-

Roman Imperial Coins.   55

rounding a large S. C. A fine, well-preserved specimen. M. B.

1244 GERMANICUS. A duplicate. Very fair. M. B.

1245 CALIGULA, A.D. 37; the goddess Piety seated, ins. surrounding, in ex. PIETAS; rev. a temple, six columns, figures before it making a sacrifice. S. C. Poor, but rare. G. B.

1246 —— Head to left; rev. Vesta seated, in left hand a wand, in right a wreath, above VESTA S—C. A very beautiful specimen, dark green patina, very choice. M. B.

1247 —— A duplicate in all respects, but preservation not as fine. M. B.

1248 —— Two specimens; reverses different. Fair. M. B.   2 pieces

1249 —— Obv. a hand, titles surrounding; rev. ins. S. C. in centre. Very good. S. B.   2 pieces

1250 CLAUDIUS, A.D. 41; head to left; TI CLAVDIVS, CÆSAR AVG, etc.; rev. Liberty holding a cap in right hand, LIBERTAS, AVGVSTA. Fine and well preserved. M. B.

1251 —— A duplicate, but not as good. M. B.

1252 NERO, A.D. 54; head; rev. Rome seated on a pile of arms. G. B.

1253 —— Head laureate and one crowned; rev. Rome seated as above and temple of Ianus. Both fine and interesting types. M. B.   2 pieces

1254 —— Reverses different. Very good. M. B.   3 pieces

1255 —— In poor condition. M. B.   3 pieces

1256 —— Head; rev. a tree and altar; rev. an altar; rev. a seated figure; rev. a temple. Very interesting and good lot. S. B.   5 pieces

1257 VESPASIAN, A.D. 69; head to right; rev. Fortune standing with cornucopia and rudder, FORTUNÆ REDVCI. Fine and rare. G. B.

1258 —— Head crowned, ins. as before; rev. Rome seated on armor holding a wreath. Extremely fine and rare. M. B.

1259 —— Head and ins.; rev. a female seated under a palm tree S. C. (JVDEA) CAPTA. Fair for this rare and much sought for type. M. B.

1260 —— Head; rev. Felicity standing; rev. an Eagle on a globe; rev. Rome seated. Fair, M. B.   3 pieces

1261 TITUS, A.D. 79; head to right and laureate; rev. a standing figure, S. C. Fine and rare. G. B.

1262 —— Head to r. crowned; rev. Felicity standing, S. C. FELICITAS, PVBLICA. Very fine and rare. M. B.

1263 DOMITIAN, A.D., 81; head crowned to right; rev. Fortune standing, S. C. FORTVNAE AVGVSTI. Fine and rare. M. B.

1264 —— Rev. the goddess Moneta standing with scales; rev. Concordia seated; rare reverses, one very fine. Rare. M. B. 2 pieces

1265 —— Rev. a crow on an olive branch; rev. a cow; rev. a basket holding five heads of wheat; rev. a tree; rev. an altar; rev. a cap of liberty, S. C. etc. A lot of very interesting little coins, worthy of special notice, and finely patinated. S. B. 9 pieces

1266 NERVA, A.D. 96; head to right and ins.; rev. two hands clasped, CONCORDIA EXERCITVM. Poor, but rare. M. B.

1267 TRAJAN, A.D. 98; head laureate to right; rev. a seated figure, S. C.; a fine, bold, and expressive obverse. Fine. G. B.

1268 —— Head to right, ins. as above; rev. a standing figure sacrificing, S. C. P. M. T. R. COS III. Extremely fine. G. B.

1269 —— Head to right; rev. the Emperor seated on a raised platform, a kneeling figure in front, personifying Parthia, ins. (REX-PARTHIS) DATVS; S.C. in ex.; fair and very interesting reverse. G. B.

1270 —— Head; rev. the Port of Ancona (bridge), ins. S. P. Q. R. OPTIMO PRINC. A very rare type and in good preservation. G. B.

1271 —— Rev. Abundance standing; rev. a yoke of oxen ploughing. Good. G. B. and M. B. 3 pieces

1272 —— Head; rev. Piety standing, a wreath, ins. S. C. Fine. M. B. 2 pieces

1273 —— Head; rev. a figure holding two trophies; rev. a standing figure holding the hasta and cornucopia. Good. M. B. 2 pieces

1274 HADRIAN, A.D. 117; head to right; rev. two figures, and ins. Very fine. G. B.

1275 —— Head; rev. the Emperor seated on an estrade, receiving homage from a standing figure; rev. the Emperor raising a kneeling figure. Two interesting coins in fair preservation. G. B.

1276 —— Head to right; HADRIANVS, AVG, COS III; rev. the goddess Hygeia sacrificing, SALVS AVG. Extremely fine. M. B.

1277 —— Head, ins. as before; rev. a seated figure feeding a serpent from a patera. Also extremely fine. M. B.

1278 —— Heads; rev. the genius of Spain reclining, HIS-

PANIA, S C; rev. the Emperor raising a kneeling figure (——) GALLIAE, good ; two types seldom met with, very rare. M. B. 2 pieces

1279 HADRIAN, A.D. 117 ; rev. a club ; rev. a boar ; rev. a wreath, etc. 4 interesting coins, well patinated. S. B. 5 pieces

1280 ANTINOUS ; head to the left, ANTINOOC. EROC ; rev. a ram, in front a caduceus, and ins. surrounding. Very interesting and *rare*, struck probably at Smyrna. MEDALLION. Size, 25

1281 ANTONINUS PIUS, A.D. 138 ; head bearded and laureate to right ; rev. S. C. the Emperor standing. An extremely fine coin, sharp and perfectly patinated. G. B.

1282 —— Head and legend as above ; rev. the Emperor in a chariot drawn by four horses ; in ex. COS IIII. S. C. Very fine specimen with perfect green patination, very rare type. G. B.

1283 —— Obv. head with titles ; rev. head of Marcus Aurelius ; obv. head ; rev. a temple of four stories, CONSECRATIO. Two very interesting types. G. B. 2 pieces

1284 —— Heads to right ; rev. Justice standing with scales ; rev. female standing with children, PIETATI, AVG. Very good. G. B. 2 pieces

1285 —— Rev. HONORI, AVG, female standing ; rev. LIBERTAS, female standing. Very good. G. B. 2 pieces

1286 —— Rev. a winged Victory holding a spear ; rev. a standing female holding a lyre. Good. G. B. 2 pieces

1287 —— Head to right, crowned, and ins. ; rev. a winged Victory holding a standard, S. C. Very fine and sharp. M. B.

1288 —— Rev. in ex. ANNONA AVG, a seated female ; rev. ANNONA, AVG, a standing figure ; good and interesting reverses. M. B. 2 pieces

1289 —— Rev. FORT, RED, a seated female ; rev. IMPERATOR, Romulus and Remus and the Wolf. Fine and rare. M. B. 2 pieces

1290 —— Rev. a galley ; rev. PRIMI DECEN-NALLIS within a wreath ; rev. PAX AVG, Peace standing. Very good. M. B. 3 pieces

1291 —— Head to right ; rev. S. C., three standards. Good and scarce. S. B.

1292 FAUSTINA (wife of Antoninus) ; head to right, DIVA FAVSTINA ; rev. AETERNITAS. Very fine, light green patina. G. B.

1293 FAUSTINA. Head as before; rev. female standing. Very fine, perfectly patinated. M. B.

1294 —— Veiled head of the Empress; rev. AETERNITAS, female seated on a globe. A rare type and desirable. M. B.

1295 —— Rev. AVGVSTA, female standing; rev. Eternity standing. Very good. M. B. 2 pieces

1296 MARCUS AURELIUS, A.D. 161; head laureate to right, and ins.; rev. Victory marching; rev. SALVS. AVG, Health sacrificing. Fine, and well patinated. G. B. 2 pieces

1297 —— Rev. a military figure; rev. Health standing; rev. TR, POT XIII, military figure standing. Good. G. B. 3 pieces

1298 —— Head crowned to r.; rev. S. C. Victory bearing a shield inscribed VIC-GER. Extremely fine and well preserved, with fine patina. M. B.

1299 —— As above; rev. a wreath enclosing the legend, PRIMI DECEN-NALES, COS III. Beautiful, and perfectly patinated. M. B.

1300 —— As before; rev. the Wolf and Twins, ins. surrounding. Very fine, patina perfect, struck on an oblong planchet. M. B.

1301 —— Young head to r.; rev. S. C. in a wreath. Good, and scarce. S. B.

1302 FAUSTINA (the younger); head and bust to right; rev. in the background a temple, before which is an altar, six figures surrounding, sacrificing, S. C. A very elegant medallion, not patinated. Size, 22

1303 —— Head to right; rev. AVGVST, PII, FIL, a standing female, S. C. Very fine. G. B.

1304 —— Rev. the Sacred Carpentum drawn by two Mules, in ex. S. P. Q. R. Fine and very rare type, desirable. G. B.

1305 —— Head to right; rev. a standing figure. Perfectly patinated; obverse very fine. M. B.

1306 —— Head, with very long neck; rev. VENVS, female standing; rev. a female holding a warrior by the arm, VICTRICI, S. C. Good reverses. M. B. 2 pieces

1307 LUCIUS VERUS (associated with Aurelius); head to right; rev. a large galley, the Emperor sitting in the stern of the ship; struck in commemoration of the Emperor's voyage from Rome to Athens. A very fine and very rare type, in fine preservation, reddish patina. G. B.

1308 —— Head to right; rev. HONOS, S. C., a standing figure holding a cornucopia; rev. CONSECRATIO,

the Emperor sitting on the back of an eagle. Two good coins, reverses rare. G. B. 2 pieces
LUCIUS VERUS. Rev. PIETAS, AVG, sacrificial instruments; rev. a captive seated beneath a trophy; rev. Victory crowning a trophy. Very good and interesting types. G. B. 3 pieces
—— Head; rev. a captive seated surrounded by arms, in ex. ARMEN. Very fine, and patinated. M. B.
—— Rev. a horse feeding; obv. head of Antoninus Pius; rev. head of Verus; rev. sacrificial emblems. Good and rare. M. B. 3 pieces
LUCILLA (wife of Verus); rev. female standing at an altar, S. C. Very good. G. B.
COMMODUS, A.D. 180; head to right, laureated; rev. a female holding a laurel branch, S. C. HILAR-ITAS, AVG. A very fine specimen, the head a good and very expressive portrait. G. B.
—— Head; rev. the Emperor seated on an estrade with two attendants, a third ascending a ladder, bearing offerings. Well preserved and deeply patinated, rare. G. B.
—— Head; rev. Commodus in a chariot drawn by four horses. Very good and rare reverse. G. B.
—— Head and ins. (good portrait); rev. Victory marching to right. Fine and well patinated. G. B.
—— Head to right, dressed in lion-skin head-dress (as Hercules); rev. within a wreath the club of Hercules, HERCVL, ROMAN, AVGV, S. C. In fine preservation, fine green patina, very desirable, extremely rare type. M. B.
SEPTIMUS SEVERUS, A.D. 193; head to right; rev. Severus and his two sons sacrificing at an altar; obverse fine. G. B.
—— Head and ins. as above; rev. a trophy of arms, a captive on each side, PARTHIA, VICT., etc. Good, and one other. G. B. 2 pieces
JULIA DOMNA (wife of Severus); head; rev. VESTA, Vesta seated. Fine red patina, rare. G. B.
GETA, A.D. 212; head; rev. the brothers at an altar, S. C. Fine and rare. G. B.
CARACALLA, A.D. 217; head to right, laureate; rev. figure standing holding pontifical instruments. Extremely fine and deeply patinated. G. B.
JULIA SOAMIAS, (mother of Elagabulus); head, JVLIA SOAMIAS; rev. VENVS CAELESTIS, Venus standing, a star in the r. field; bright and sharp as when struck. Very choice. S. B.

1324 SEVERUS ALEXANDER, A.D. 222; head; rev. The Sun; rev. Victory holding a wreath. Fine. G. B. 2 pieces

1325 —— Head; rev. Emperor standing holding a globe; rev. Victory holding a wreath. Fine. G. B. 2 pieces

1326 —— Rev. Mars Ultor; rev. ANNONA AVGVSTI, female standing; rev. figure holding a palm branch. Very good. G. B. 3 pieces

1327 —— Head; rev. a bouquet of 6 heads of wheat. Poor, but rare type. M. B.

1328 —— Head; rev. female holding a standard; rev. Providence standing. M. B. 2 pieces

1329 JULIA MAMAEA (mother of Alexander); head; rev. Felicity standing, leaning on a short column. Fine, light green patina. G. B.

1330 —— Head; rev. female standing, bird to left, IVNO. Fine and rare. G B.

1331 MAXIMINUS, A.D. 238; head to right; rev. VICTORIA AVG, Victory holding a wreath. Very fine. G. B.

1332 —— Head; rev. Liberality standing holding cornucopia. Very fine and patinated. M. B.

1333 MAXIMUS, A.D. 238; head ; MAXIMVS CAES; rev. PRINCIPI IVVENTATIS, Maximus near two ensigns. Good and rare. G. B.

1334 PAULINA (wife of Maximus), veiled head of the Empress; rev. CONSECRATIO, Paulina seated on an eagle's back, S. C.; struck in honor of her consecration and apotheosis. Fine and extremely rare. G. B.

1335 PUPIENUS, A.D. 238; head to right, IMP CAES M CLOD, PVPIENVS, AVG; rev. CONCORDIA AVGG, Concord seated. Very fair, extremely rare. G. B.

1336 GORDIANU PIUS III., A.D. 238; head; rev. the Emperor seated, holding a branch. Fine. G. B.

1337 —— Head; rev. Armed figure charging; rev. VICTORIA, Victory holding a wreath. Both fine. G. B. 2 pieces

1338 —— Head; rev. the King with three attendants, giving to a third; rev. the King on horseback, AETERNITAS, AVGG. Two good coins, reverses rare. G. B. 2 pieces

1339 —— Head; rev. MARS-VLTOR; rev. FORTIVNA ; rev. LIBERALITAS; rev. MARS PROPVGNATORI. All interesting and good. G. B. 4 pieces

1340 —— Head; rev. Fortitude standing. Fine. M. B.

PHILIP (the Arab), A.D. 244; head, IMP IVLIVL PHILIPPVS AVG; rev. FIDES EXERCITVS, four standards. Very good. G. B.
—— Head; rev. SAECVLARES AVGG, a stag. Very good. G. B.
—— Head crowned; rev. a lion, and one billon. Fair. S. B. 2 pieces
MARCIA OTACILIA (wife of Philip); head; rev. CONCORDIA, Concord seated. Extremely fine, with perfect patination of dark green. Very desirable. G. B.
PHILIP II. (son of the Arab); head; rev. IVENTVS AVG. the Prince on horseback; rev. PRINCIPII IVENT, the Prince standing, holding a spear. Good and fine. G. B. 2 pieces
—— Head; rev. a seated figure holding a ball. Very fine. M. B.
TRAJANUS DECIUS, A.D. 249; head laureate; rev. VICTORIA, Victory holding a wreath. Very fine, with deep green patina. G. B.
—— Head, reverses different. Fine, with black patina. G. B. 4 pieces
ETRUSCILLA (wife of Decius); head; rev. FECVNDITAS AVG, female with child and cornucopia. Fine and rare type. G. B.
TREBONIANUS GALLUS, A.D. 251; head laureate; rev. Felicity standing, S. C.; rev. AETERNITAS, Eternity standing. One very fine. G. B. 2 pieces
VOLUSIANUS, A.D. 254; head laureate; rev. CONCORDIA, concord seated S. C.; rev. Abundance standing with cornucopia and wreath. Very good. G. B. 2 pieces
GALLIENUS, A.D. 253; head; rev. VIRTVS AVG, warrior standing, spear in hand; square coin. Fine and rare. G. B.
—— Head with radiated crown; rev. SALVS, Health standing; rev. NEPTVNO, a sea horse. One extremely fine. S. B. 2 pieces
POSTUMUS, A.D. 258; head with radiated crown; rev. a standing figure. Very rare in 1st Brass. G. B.
—— Head as before; rev. LAETITIA, a galley. Very fine. S. B.
VICTORINUS, A.D. 267; head; rev. PAX AVG, Peace standing, a star behind, and one other. S. B. 2 pieces
CLAUDIUS GOTHICUS, A.D. 278; head crowned; rev. an eagle, and one other. Fine. S. B. 2 pieces

1358 CLAUDIUS GOTHICUS; rev. standing figure. Fine. S. B. 2 pieces
1359 QUINTILLUS, A.D. 270; head; figure holding a standard; rev. Faith standing. S. B. 2 pieces
1360 AURELIAN, A.D. 270; head crowned; rev. a warrior. S. B. 3 pieces
1361 SEVERINA (wife of Aurelian); head; rev. IVNO REGINA, Juno standing with hasta. Fair, but very rare. M. B.
1362 TETRICUS, A.D. 273; head to right and crowned; rev. female holding a branch. Very fine. S. B. 2 pieces
1363 —— Same; reverses different. Very good. S. B. 3 pieces
1364 TACITUS, A. D. 275; head crowned; rev. Providence standing; rev. SALVS PVBLICA. Very fine. S. B. 2 pieces
1365 FLORIANUS, A.D. 276; head crowned, IMP FLORIANVS, AVG; rev. JOVI STATORI, Jupiter standing. Very fine. S. B.
1366 PROBUS, A.D. 276; crowned head; rev. a quadriga. Very fine, tin coating still remaining. S. B. 4 pieces
1367 —— As before; reverses all different. Very fine. S. B. 5 pieces
1368 —— As before; reverses all different. Very fine. S. B. 6 pieces
1369 —— As above; reverses all different. Very fine. S. B. 6 pieces
1370 CARUS, A.D. 282; head crowned; rev. figure holding a standard. Fine. S. B. 2 pieces
1371 DIOCLETIAN, A.D. 285; head laureate; rev. GENIO POPVLI ROMANI, standing figure. Extremely fine. M. B.
1372 —— Same; rev. Justice standing; rev. standing figure. Very fine. M. B. 3 pieces
1373 —— Same; rev. as before. Very fine. S. B. 3 pieces
1374 MAXIMIANUS (Hercules), A.D. 286; head, IMP MAXIMIANUS; rev. warrior marching. Extremely fine. M. B. 2 pieces
1375 —— As before; rev. Moneta with scales; rev. Genius of Roma, etc. A fine lot. M. B. 3 pieces
1376 —— As before; revs. differing. A fine lot, the original coating of tin remaining. S. B. 6 pieces
1377 HELENA (wife of Constantius Chlorus); head; HELENA AVGVSTA; rev. SECVRITAS REIPVBLICA, a female standing holding a branch. Very beautiful and perfect, green as an emerald. S. B.

1378 HELENA. As before; reverses different. Extremely fine. S. B. 2 pieces
1379 GALERIUS MAXIMIANUS, A.D. 305; Head laureate; rev. GENIO POPULI, figure standing. Extremely fine. M. B.
1380 —— Same; reverses differing. Very fine. M. B. 3 pieces
1381 MAXENTIUS, A.D. 306; head laureate; rev. female holding the hasta. Extremely fine. M. B.
1382 LICINIUS, A.D. 313; bearded head to right; rev. the Emperor standing. Very fine. M. B.
1383 —— As before; rev. Iovi Conservatori, and one other. Very fine. S. B. 2 pieces
1384 CONSTANTINE 1st (The Great), A.D. 306; head laureate to right; rev. Genio Populi Romani. Very fine. M. B.
1385 —— As above; rev. head with rays, SOLI, N VICTO COMITI. Very fine, unusual reverse, rare. M. B.
1386 —— Veiled head of the Emperor; the King with upstretched hands, in a quadriga; one of his consecration coins. Beautiful and very rare. S. B.
1387 CRISPUS; head; rev. an altar; rev. a wreath; rev. an altar with an offering on it. Very beautiful. S. B. 3 pieces
1388 HELENA (daughter of Constantine the Great); head; rev. RX. PVBLICA, standing female. Very pretty little coin, and very rare. S. B.
1389 CONSTANTIN II, A.D. 337; head to right; a wreath VOT X; rev. an altar; rev. Apollo, etc., etc. A very beautiful lot. S. B. 8 pieces
1390 MAGNENTIUS, A.D. 350; head to right; rev. two Victories upholding a shield, inscribed VOT V, MVLT, X. Very sharp and fine. S. B.
1391 VALENS, A.D. 364; head; rev. a Victory, SECVRITAS REIPVBLICAE. Very fine, and patinated. S. B.
1392 ARCADIUS, A.D. 395; head; rev. soldier standing, CONCORDIA, etc. Very good. S. B. 2 pieces
1393 CONSTANS II. A.D. 407; head; rev. a bird standing on a globe; rev. Victory, etc. All fine. S. B. 4 pieces

Ancient Coins Unclassified.

Copper.

1394 MOORISH, with ancient characters on both sides. Well patinated and curious coins. S. B. 6 pieces

64 *Ancient Coins Unclassified.*

1395 MISCELLANEOUS; helmet; rev. owl; head; rev. cuirass; helmet; rev. Caduceus, S. C. All fine. S. B.   6 pieces

1396 —— Coins of the lower Roman Empire. Very good lot.   15 pieces

1397 —— Roman coins. G. B. and M. B. Fair condition.   50 pieces

1398 —— " " " Fair condition.   50 pieces

1399 —— " " " Fair condition   50 pieces

1400 —— " " " Fair condition   54 pieces

1401 —— " " S. B. Poor.   50 pieces

1402 —— " " " "   50 pieces

1403 GREEK coins of Hiero II.; Agathocles; Ptolemy II.; Phintias (tyrant of Agrigentum); Syracuse, etc., etc. Fine to poor.   12 pieces

1404 COPTIC coins, with unknown legends, Tunny fish, dolphin, horse running, etc.; some with Latin and etruscan inscriptions. All quite uncommon.   17 pieces

1405 ROMAN Imperial coins in wrappers, with description in full; have been kept together so long as a collection, that we will sell them as they are. Among them are several that are very rare; we will specify a Decursio of Nero, one of Claudius; rev. equestrian statue; several with two and three heads; a Vitellius, first size, which we believe to be ancient; one of Claudius, with heads of Drusus and Germanicus. A collector desiring to purchase this lot ought to see them, as it is only by so doing that an intelligent judgment of their character and value can be formed.   68 pieces

Silver.

1406 GREEK Drachma of Chalcis, and two others.   3 pieces

1407 DENARIUS of the Procilia family, with Juno Lanuvium on the rev.; others of the Calpurnia, Tituria, Æmilia, Satriena, etc., etc. All uncommon and good examples.   10 pieces

1408 —— Similar lot, Antonia, Sentia, Tatia, Papia, Vibia, etc.   10 pieces

1409 —— Similar.   10 pieces

1410 —— Similar.   10 pieces

1411 CALIPHS; a fine lot of broad coins of irregular shape, each containing about 25 cents worth of silver. Cufic inscription.   4 pieces

1412 —— Similar lot, about half the size of last.   5 pieces

(End of 3d days sale)

AMERICAN COLONIAL AND STATE COINS AND TOKENS.

Massachusetts.

1413 N. E. Shilling; obv. N. E.; rev. XII; both in a square incusum. Authentic, and one of the best examples existing. Very rare. Size, 20
1414 N. E. Threepence; same type; (rev. III.) Size, 12
1415 PINE TREE Shilling, 1652, MASATHVSETS, IN*; neat, compact tree, and well-formed letters; rev. NEW ENGLAND, AN. DOM.* 1652, XII. Entirely uncirculated and beautiful.; in this condition extremely rare. Size, 19
1416 Same; large oval tree, and heavy letters. A variety that strikes the eye at once as remarkable; in the best preservation. Size, 18
1416*—— Another; very fine, with oval planchet.
1417 Same; tall tree, pointed top; very large letters and figures. Very fine and rare. Size, 18
1418 Same; similar tree, in circle of smaller dots. Equally fine. Size, 18
1419 Same; more like 1417. Good example.
1420 Same; varieties, clipped and imperfect. 2 pieces
1421 Same; a variety punctuated by a single dot; oblique branches and upright spines; long base under the trunk of the tree. Good example. Size, 18
1422 Same; a variety of the smaller shillings, in which the W in legend consists of two V's not united, thus, V V; small letters. Very fine. Size, 15
1423 Same; united rev.; nearly as fine. Same size.
1424 Same; variety in form of letters and punctuated. About like last.
1425 YEW TREE (?) shilling; two shoots at the root of the tree. Fine and rare. Size, 18
1426 PINE TREE sixpence; same date; dot on each side of trunk; never in circulation. Very fine and sharp impression.
1427 Same; without dots to right and left of tree; thinner planchet. Very fine.
1428 PINE TREE threepence; same date. Fine.
1429 Same; a variety. Very fine.
1430 OAK TREE shilling; 1652; reverse die broken; full size and weight, but imperfect impression. Very rare. Size, 18
1431 Same; die less broken and smaller; better *impression*. Fine tree; very rare. Size, 16

1432 OAK TREE shilling; 1652; *very* large letters; I think the willow tree; no trunk distinguishable, although a fair impression. Size, 17

1433 Same; the oak tree, with broad trunk; nicked planchet, but fine impression. Size, 18

1434 Same; smaller, and of a poorer quality of silver; perhaps a counterfeit of the period. Fine.

1435 OAK TREE sixpence; extremely fine, nearly uncirculated coin. Very rare. Size, 13

1436 OAK TREE threepence. Fine. Size, 11¼

1437 Same; punctuated by a rosette. Fine and rare.

1438 OAK TREE twopence, 1662. Extremely fine and perfect impression. Very rare.

1439 Same; marked variety. Very fine.

1440 CENT; MASSACHUSETTS, 1787; eagle displayed, olive branch and bundle of eight arrows in talons; rev. COMMONWEALTH, Indian standing with arrow and bow. Extremely fine and uncirculated impression, with only marks of the wear inevitable from the friction of the Cabinet drawer; very rare.

1441 HALF-CENT; same date; match to preceding, but with eleven arrows. Entirely uncirculated.

1442 Another cent and half-cent; same date and variety. Very fine. 2 pieces

1443 CENT; the eagle holding *thirteen* arrows; same date. Very fine; rare.

1444 HALF-CENT; eagle holding *nine* arrows. Fair.

1445 CENT of 1788. Extremely fine.

1446 HALF-CENT; same date. Uncirculated.

1447 Another cent and half-cent of this date. Very fine. 2 pieces

1448 Others; 1788; cents (2) and half-cent. Good. 3 pieces

Maryland.

1449 LORD BALTIMORE shilling; CÆCILIVS: DNS: TERRÆ-MARIÆ: &CT, bust to left; rev. CRESITE, ET: MVLTIPLICANINI, shield crowned, at the sides X——II.; uncommonly fine and strong impression. Very desirable and rare.

1450 Same; sixpence V——I. Equally fine and rare.

1451 Same; groat I——V. Fully equal, and more rare than the other denomination.

[If this set could remain together it would grace any cabinet in the country. I do not remember to have catalogued another equal in all respects.]

CHALMERS shilling; Annapolis, 1783. Very fine.
Same; sixpence pierced and filled. Very fine and rare.
Same; threepence. Uncirculated; rare.
   [A beautiful set and should remain together.]
Duplicate shilling. Very fine.
LORD BALTIMORE penny; copied by W. Idler, with his card thereon; silver proof. Rare.
Same in copper; proof.
Others, silver and copper; same.   2 pieces

The Carolinas.

ELEPHANT half-penny; 1694; "God preserve Carolina and the Lord's proprietors." In only fair condition, but very rare.
   [A very desirable piece.]

Louisiana.

COPPER of LOUIS XV.; COLONIES FRANCOISES, 1721; two L's crossed and crowned. Very fine.
Same of 1722. Equally good.
Same; 1767; perfect example; not counterstamped. Very fine.
Same, with R. F. on rev. Good example.
Same; 1722 and 1767, with counterstamp.   2 pieces
Others, same as last.   2 pieces

Virginia.

CENT of 1773; beautiful proof of the full cent with milled rim, struck in collar. Rare.
HALF-PENNY, same date; large and small planchet. Ordinary.   2 pieces
Others. Same.   2 pieces
SHILLING; 1774; obv. GEORGIVS III. DEI GRATIE, bust, laureate; rev. Virginia arms crowned. Nearly proof and one of the rarest coins in the colonial series. (Only two others known)

New York.
(All Cents.)

NOVA CONSTELATIO (one L); blunt rays, U. S. in caps; 1783. Extra fine.
Same; same date; larger planchet. Very fine.
Same; pointed rays, heavier wreath. Extra fine.
Same; 1785; U. S. in script., blunt rays. Very fine.
Same; 1785; pointed rays. Uncirculated; rare.
Same; a variety, equally fine.

1476 IMMUNE COLUMBIA; 1785; Liberty sitting on square seat; rev. Nova Constellatio (two Ls); nearly uncirculated. Very rare.

1477 IMMUNE COLUMBIA; same date; rev. another variety of the Nova Constellatio; obv. fine, reverse poor. Rare to excess.

1478 IMMUNE COLUMBIA; 1785; rev. "Vermon Auctori," with head of George III.? In fair preservation and excessively rare.

1479 Same, with reverse of "Georgius III. Rex," head as before. Same condition and equally rare.

1480 NEW YORK Washington cent; 1786; obv. bust of Washington, NON VI VIRTUTE VICI; rev. Liberty seated, NEO EBO RACENCIS. Uncirculated, but with original marks remaining on planchet; not perfectly struck up; perfectly round, with finely milled edge, which is not usual. Excessively rare.

1481 IMMUNIS COLUMBIA; 1786; Liberty seated on *globe*; rev. shield, E PLURIBUS UNUM; nearly proof; a beautiful coin, with perfectly milled rim. Very rare.

1482 GEORGE CLINTON; 1787; bust of the first Governor of New York; rev. arms of the State, EXCELSIOR; good impression. Very rare and valuable.

1483 LIBER NATUS LIBERTATEM DEFENDO; Indian standing; rev. "Excelsior," arms of the State. In only fair condition, but rare to excess and desirable.

1484 EXCELSIOR; rev. eagle displayed (the eagle on crest standing to r.); dark, but sharp. Desirable.

1485 IMMUNIS COLUMBIA; 1787; Liberty seated on globe; rev. eagle displayed, and motto E PLURIBUS UNUM same as on last. Uncirculated; rare.

1486 Same; inferior to last, but fine.

1487 NOVA EBORAC; mailed bust laureate. large head; rev. Liberty seated to left, VIRT ET LIB; a variety almost unknown to collectors; as rare as the "Neo Eboracensis." In excellent condition and valuable.

1488 Same; usual type; rev. Liberty seated to left. Very fine; never in circulation.

1489 Same; Liberty seated to *right*. Equally fine; rare.

1490 PAIR of the Nova Eboracs; Liberty r. and l. Never in circulation. 2 pieces

Vermont.

1491 VERMONT'S RES PUBLICA; landscape at sunrise, eight trees; below plough, 1785; rev. "Quarta Decima Stella," blunt rays. Very good; rare.

1492 Same; another. Not as good.

American Colonial, State Coins, Tokens. 69

1493 VERMONTIS, etc.; only variety in title ; same date. Not fine, but good for the piece.
1494 VERMONTENSIUM ; 1786 ; seven trees. Fine.
1495 Same ; eight trees. Very good.
1496 AUCTORI VERMON ; baby head, with the usual notch in planchet. Fair.
1497 Same, without notch. Very rare ; fair.
1498 VERMON AUCTORI ; laureated head, copied from English halfpenny, 1787. Fair.
1499 Same, 1788 ; large planchet. Good for variety.
1500 Duplicates, several varieties. Ordinary. 4 pieces
1501 VERMON AUCTORI, 1788 ; small planchet. Fine for variety, scarce.
1502 Same ; rev. Britannia and another. 3 pieces

Connecticut.

1503 GRANBY copper, 1757 ; deer standing to l. ; rev. three hammers crowned ; black and pierced. Rare.
1504 Gov. BRADFORD head, 1765 ; rev. Liberty seated ; a faint, but uncirculated impression. Rare.
1505 NEGRO head and others, laureated, facing to right ; mailed busts. All in good condition. 4 pieces
1506 LAUREATED heads to l., busts mailed, 1786. Varieties, all in good condition. 6 pieces
1507 SMALL head to r., 1787 ; rev. "Et Lib Inde." Rare.
1508 LAUGHING effigies ; broad laurel wreath, 1787. Fine. 2 pieces
1509 BUST with *horned* coat of mail, 1787. Fine. 2 pieces
1510 DRAPED bust to l., large and small letters ; several varieties. Fine lot, 1787. 5 pieces
1511 Same, 1788. Good lot. 5 "

New Jersey.

1512 HORSE head above plough, 1786 ; rev. *broad* shield ; nearly uncirculated. Rare.
1513 Others, varieties of this date. Good. 3 pieces
1514 ONE of 1787 ; large planchet rim finely milled. *Extremely* fine, rare.
1515 Others, 1787 ; thick and thin, large planchet. Good. 5 pieces
1516 Cents of same date, small planchets ; several varieties, one pierced. Fine lot. 5 pieces
1517 LARGE cents of 1788. Fair. 2 "
1518 DOG type, same date ; broken die. Fine and very rare.
1519 Another ; distinct variety. Very good, rare.

70 *American Colonial, State Coins, Tokens.*

1520 HORSE HEAD to l., same date; extremely sharp and fine, but dark. Very rare.
1521 Another. Not as fine.

Kentucky.

1522 HAND holding scroll; thereon, "Our cause is just;" rev. thirteen stars arranged as a pyramid; lettered edge, "Payable in London, Lancaster, or Bristol." Uncirculated.
1523 Same; edge *engrailed.* Uncirculated and extremely rare.
1524 Same; edge plain. Uncirculated.
1525 MYDDELTON cent or token, 1796, "British settlement Kentucky;" Liberty receiving two children from a foreign mother, anchor near. Brilliant proof, rare.

Rosa Americana's and Woods' Tokens.

1526 TWOPENCE (penny size), without date; obv. laureated bust of George I.; rev. full-blown rose UTILE-DULCI on a schedule; strictly uncirculated; an extremely beautiful example. Rare. Size, 20
1527 PENNY (halfpenny size), 1722; same type, not much worn, but dark. Size, 16½
1528 HALFPENNY (farthing size), same type, 1722. *Very fine,* rare.
1529 Same, legend "Rosa *Ameri*"; splendid uncirculated impression. Very rare.
1530 PENNY (halfpenny), rose *crowned.* Good.
1531 HALFPENNY (farthing), beautiful uncirculated example, same type. Very rare.
1532 PENNY and halfpenny; plain rose. Very good. 2 pieces
1533 Same; variety. 3 "
1534 IMPRESSION on type metal of the unique large Rosa Americana with the motto in *field.* Size, 24
1535 WOODS' halfpenny, with the harp to left or Hibernia; pierced, 1722. 2 pieces
1536 Same, 1723; nearly uncirculated. Rare.
1537 FARTHING and halfpennies; some fine. 8 pieces

Miscellaneous.

1537* AUCTORI Plebis; rev. Hispaniola and R. Campin's card halfpenny, 1736 and 1794. 2 pieces
1538 VOCE POPULI; rev. Hibernia, 1760; varieties, halfpennies. Very fine. 3 pieces

American Colonial, State Coins, Tokens. 71

1539 GEORGIUS TRIUMPHE; rev. Voce Populi, 1783. Very fine.
1540 Same; finer than last, pierced.
1541 PITT TOKEN; "No stamps," 1766; bust in wig; rev. ship "America." Extremely fine, rare.
1542 Same, silver-plated. Very good.
1543 NORTH American Token; rev. ship with Columbia farthings. Fine lot. 8 pieces
1544 LONDON ELEPHANT, halfpennies, one very fine. 2 "
1545 CASTOR LAND TOKEN by *Du Vivier;* obv. head of Ceres, FRANCO-AMERICANA COLONIA, in ex. "Castorland, 1796"; rev. maple tree yielding sap, Ceres standing near; edge plain. Fine proof, bronze. Size, 21
1546 Same in silver, edge milled. Splendid proof.
1547 Another in silver, from different die. Brilliant proof.
1548 Franklin cent; obv. sun and dial, FUGIO, 1787; in ex. "Mind your business"; rev. WE ARE ONE, in the centre of a blazing sun, circumscribed by a chain of 13 links, on each of which is inscribed the name of an original State. In very fair condition and *Presque* unique, only one other, so far as the writer's information extends, being known.
1549 FRANKLIN Press halfpenny, London, 1796. Uncirculated.
1550 MARTHA WASHINGTON half disme, 1792; bust, LIBERTY PARENT OF SCIENCE AND INDUSTRY; rev. eagle with expanded wings, etc. *Very fine* example, rare.
1551 WASHINGTON "Small Eagle" cent of 1791, extremely fine. Scarce.
1552 LIBERTY AND SECURITY Washington penny, without date. Uncirculated.
1553 BAR CENT; original. Poor.
1554 MOTT'S Token, 1789; original thick and thin planchet. 2 pieces
1555 TALBOT, Allum and Lee cent, 1794; varieties: one with Howard the philanthropist, one with head of Earl Howe, and one with two dates; rev. stork; two uncirculated and bright. Rare lot. 3 pieces
1556 Same, 1795. Perfectly uncirculated. 2 "

[From new dies, copies, and imitations of rare colonial.]

1557 SOMMER Islands shilling in brass; hog; rev. ship. Fine proof.
1558 Same; rev. Dickeson's coin and medal safe, etc., copper. Fine proof.

1559 Wyatt's Good Samaritan shilling; rev. oak tree; perfect impression on *thick* planchet, pure silver. Rare.
1560 Same, thin planchet. Rare.
1561 Bolen's "Inimica Tyrannis," etc., 1785, with "Non Dependens Status." Fine proof.   2 pieces
1562 Another "Non-dependens," with bar cent.   2 "

American Medals in Various Metals.

Vernon Series—Brass.

1563 Varieties; The Hon. Edward Vernon, Vernon and Brown, Vernon and Ogle, etc., etc.; no duplicates, various sizes, one oval. In very fine condition. 20 pieces.
1564 Another lot; on one, the Devil walking off with Sir Robert. Equally fine lot, and it is believed very free from duplicates.   20 pieces
1565 Similar lot, large and small.   14 "

Rhode Island.

1566 —— Obv. Map of a small State, with four rows of soldiers crossing it; to l. ships, to r. boats filled with troops: others empty; rev. Flag-ship of Admiral Howe 1778–1779, silver-plated. Original and very rare.
    Size, 21
1567 Same, in brass, still a variety. The ornament under the ship having been cut from the reverse of the one first described. Uncirculated.
1568 Same, in tin. Uncirculated.
1569 Same as 1566; the ornament having been cut from the reverse, but in brass. Uncirculated.

Peace Medals.

1570 Libertas Americana, 1783; Louis XVI. on his throne, pointing to the new American shield which a female is hanging on a high post surmounted by a liberty cap; rev. Minerva holding a cordon of shields. COMMVNI CONSENSV; tin, with copper plug. Fine proof.
    Size, 29
1571 Duplicate. Uncirculated.
1572 Libera Soror, 1782; Minerva joining hands with the genius of America under a meridian sun, between them a lighted altar; rev. Unicorn dashing against a rock. TYRANNIS VIRTUTE REPVLSA. *Extremely* fine and rare. Silver.   Size, 28
1573 Faustissimo Foedere Junctæ, 1782; Fame on clouds supporting crown and two shields; rev. Mercury descending, placing a crown on a trophy standing on a monument; on scroll, PRO-DRO-MVS, Anchor, Cock,

American Medals in various Metals. 73

and Cornucopia near ; ships in the offing. Fine proof. Silver, and rare. Size, 29

1574 FAUSTISSIMO FOEDERE JUNCTÆ, 1872 ; smaller ; equally fine. Size, 22 — *Strobridge*

1575 PEACE Medal by *Calker*, 1782 ; three figures standing ; Mercury descending. DE VER EENIG STAATEN VAN NOORD AMERICA. Fine proof ; silver. Size, 28 — *Parish*

1576 NEDERLAND VERKLAARD AMERICA VRY, 1782 ; Liberty standing ; rev. merchandise on dock under two flags, sloop behind. Uncirculated ; silver. Size, 22 — "

1577 HOEZEE : DE BRIT RUIMT ZEE (whatever that may mean) ; two ships in action, one with British flag ; rev. ins. in 8 lines, 1781 ; one of the series of Dutch American Peace medals ; silver. Very fine. Size, 19 — *Holland*

1578 To commemorate the Treaty signed at Ghent, 1814 ; Peace standing on a globe, "On Earth peace, goodwill to men" ; rev. ins., etc. ; bronze ; good condition and rare. Size, 29 — *Parish*

1579 Similar, in tin. Very fine. Same size — *Nichols*

1580 PEACE SPREADS HER INFLUENCE O'ER THE ATLANTCI SHORE ; Peace standing ; rev. "Concord between Great Britain and America," by Mills ; bronze. Uncirculated, rare. Size, 26 — *Warner*

MISCELLANEOUS.

1581 PITT medal, "The man who having saved the Parent," etc. Original, silver ; extremely fine. Size, 26 — *Rugg*

1582 Same, in copper ; proof. — *Ahlborn*

1583 Same, restruck ? ; silver, proof, thick planchet. Size, 26

1584 PENN INDIAN medal ; "Let us look to the Most High, who blessed our fathers with peace ;" bust of George II. ; rev. Penn and Indian seated, the former pointing with a calumet to the sun, etc. Proof impression from broken die ; in bronze. Size, 28

1585 PENN commemorative medal ; bust ; rev. Penn and Indian standing, "By deeds of Peace," etc. Born 1644, died 1718 ; bronze. Very fine. Size, 26 — *James*

1585* GERMANTOWN medal, Oct. 4, 1777 ; rev. attack on the town, by *Milton*. Original, in bronze, pierced. Fine and rare to excess. Size, 28 — *Nelson*

1586 COLUMBIA AND WASHINGTON EXPLORING VESSELS ; view of the ships ; rev. "Fitted at Boston, N. America, for the Pacific ocean," etc., etc. ; bronze, in very good condition ; rare. Size, 26 — *Holland*

1587 FULTON medal ; SACRED TO THE MEMORY OF ROBERT FULTON, ONE OF THE MOST, etc. ; — *Nichols* rev. large steamboat, no inscription. Very fine medal, nearly proof and excessively rare ; tin.   Size, 34

[No. 2185 of the McCoy catalogue, where it was described as "of the highest variety, probably unique."]

1588 ERIE CANAL MEDAL, by *Thomason;* "Union of Erie with the Atlantic," Neptune and A Satyr; rev. arms of New York and inscription ; tin proof. Scarce.   Size, 52

1589 Same, but of reduced size, and struck in silver. Extremely fine. *C. C. Wright.*   Size, 28

1590 NEW HAVEN commemorative medal ; second centenary, "Quinnipiack 1638, New Haven 1838"; fine proof in bronze. Rare.   Size, 36

1591 Same; nickel-plated; proof.

1592 TRISTRAM COFFIN, 1642 ; figure in the full costume of that date standing on a pedestal, cane in hand : THE FIRST OF HIS RACE THAT SETTLED IN AMERICA ; rev. four hands joined. Extremely fine, bronze, silver-plated ; rare.   Size, 34

[Purchased at the Hoffman sale April, 1866. No. 1606 of the Catalogue cost $7.50.]

1593 CROTON AQUEDUCT, to commemorate its completion 4th July, 1842 ; bronze, thick planchet ; proof.   Size, 34

1594 Same, silver-plated; also proof. Very rare.

1595 Same, in tin ; proof.

1596 Same, with different reverse ; plain field inclosed by palm and oak branches ; tin, in very fine condition and very rare.   Same size

1597 NEW YORK CRYSTAL PALACE ; to commemorate the Exhibition of 1853, a fine representation of the building ; rev. a globe surrounded by representative figures of Europe, Asia, Africa, and America ; fine proof in tin.   Size, 48

1598 Same ; rev. view of the "Latting observatory, N. York, extreme height 350 feet," also a comparative view of the Crystal Palace and Croton Reservoir, an excessively rare medal from the McCoy collection, No. 2182 of the catalogue, where it is described as "excessively rare, perhaps unique"; tin. Very fine.   Size, 34

1599 Same ; rev. "The first pillar was erected," etc. ; fine proof (from same collection as last), tin.   Size, 33

1599* Duplicate ; same in all respects.

1600 Same ; rev. "Destroyed by fire Oct. 5, 1858, in 40 minutes." The American Institute occupying it for their annual fair, 3,000 visitors present ; tin, fine proof.   Same size

American Medals in various Metals. 75

1601 KANE Medal, by *Tiffany & Co.*; Kane and companions in furs, ship and ice in the distance; rev. arms of New York, one of the supporters seated; fine proof, bronze. Size, 38   *Hazeltine*
1602 Another, same in all respects.   *Same*
1603 Same, bust; below tablet showing a view of ships in the ice, flags to right and left; rev. Masonic emblems. Fine proof, tin. Size, 32   "
1604 Same, bust; rev. "Born in Philadelphia, Pa., Feb. 3, 1822; Commander of the Grinnell Arctic Expedition, May 30, 1853; died Feb. 14, 1857." Tin, proof. Size, 24   "
1605 Same; obv. Kane and native Esquimo with their dogs, etc.; rev. same as 1601, except that the seated figure (Justice) holds a sword instead of balance. Bronze. Size, 52   "

[This is an original, and appears to be a cast medal. The writer has seen no other, and therefore is unable to give a better account of it.]

1606 ADVANCE AND RESCUE; "Presented by British Residents of New York to John Blinn, Quarter-Master," etc. 1851. Silver, loop removed. Fair, scarce. Size, 24   *Holland*
1607 HERNDON Medal, by *Smith & Hartman*; obv. inscription inclosed by laurel branches:—"Presented to the widow of Capt. William Lewis Herndon, U. S. Navy, by Virginia," etc.; rev. steamboat going down, Herndon on the wheel-house; splendid proof. Silver, rare. Size, 37   *Windsor*
1608 TESTIMONIAL to Captains Crichton, Low, and Stouffer, by the Corporation of the City of Philadelphia, for services to the crew and passengers of the Steamer San Francisco, January, 1854; inscription; rev. arms of the City. Fine proof, bronze. Size, 48
1609 Duplicate.
1610 SUMTER; the Citizens of the City of New York to Maj. Robert Anderson, U. S. A.; view of the bombardment of the Fort, April 12–13, 1861. Fine proof, bronze. Size, 44   *Armstrong*
1611 NEW YORK VOLUNTEERS in the Mexican War; presented by the City of New York. Bronze proof impression, not engraved. Size, 34
1612 Same in silver; presented and inscribed to Barney Harrigan. Very fine.   *Ahlborn*
1613 HUMANE Society of Mass. medal; instituted 1785; by *Schollay*; obv. cabin on a sea-coast, SUCCOUR, ship wrecked, in the distance a boat load of survivors being hauled to the beach. Fine proof from the dies, unengraved. Bronze. Size, 32   "
1614 Duplicate, equally fine.

1615 PALMETTO REGIMENT medal; awarded by South Carolina; on two shields leaning against a palmetto tree, "1846–1847," with the names of battles in the Mexican war of that period. Fine proof, bronze. Size, 32

1616 UNITED STATES AGRICULTURAL SOCIETY, 1852, by *Mitchell;* Ceres seated holding a laurel crown and sickle; around, a large wreath; the execution of uncommon excellence; rev. "Awarded to," the rest blank. Bronze, proof. Size, 48

1617 SACRAMENTO CITY Agricultural and Horticultural Fair; "Prizes presented by Warren & Son." Tin, proof. Size, 34

1618 OHIO MECHANICS' INSTITUTE, incorporated Cin. 1829. Fine proof impression in bronze, with a view of the edifice by *True.* Size, 33

1619 FREE ACADEMY, Ward medal, view of the edifice; est. 1853. Fine proof, bronze. Size, 33

1620 Same; to commemorate the changing of its name to "College of the City of New York," which was done by act of the Legislature in 1866; obv. LIGHT, LIBERTY, LAW, head with diadem and starry crown; rev. ins. Splendid medal by *Key;* bronze, proof. Size, 38

1621 MAINE CHARITABLE Mechanic Association; fine Medal by *Smith & Hartman.* Bronze. Size, 33

1622 PORTSMOUTH, VIRGINIA; medal presented by the Town Council; edifice flying the Confederate flag; on a schedule "*Palmam Qui Meruit Ferat,*" underneath, Arms of the State, flags and weapons; rev. ins. and enclosed blank. Splendid proof by *Mitchel,* bronze. Size, 40

1623 To Commemorate the great Central Fair for the U. S. Sanitary Com., Philadelphia, June, 1864, by *Paquet;* rev. wounded soldier, surgeon, and female presenting a cup. Fine proof, bronze. Size, 36

1624 Another; same in all respects.
1625 Same; triplicate.

1626 NORWICH Free Academy; "Newton Perkins' Medal, 1857," by *S. & H.;* obv. fine head of Minerva; proof, bronze. Size, 32

1627 PENNSYLVANIA Volunteers, Gettysburg, 1863; arms of the State; rev. inscription and trophies. Fine proof, silver. Size, 24

1628 MONNIER METALLURGICAL COMPANY; "A medal struck from the first copper produced in Colorado, 1866"; view of smelting works; below, sledge hammer and pickaxe crossed. Splendid proof, rare. Size, 40

1629 TELEGRAPHIC CABLE Medal, to commemorate the laying of the first cable between Europe and America, 1858, by *Tiffany & Co.*; from the Chamber of Commerce and citizens of New York. Proof, bronze. Size, 44 *Proskey*

1630 Same event; different medal by same, on thick planchet. Bronze, proof. Size, 38 *Holland*

1631 NASSAU WATER WORKS; to celebrate the introduction of water in the city of Brooklyn, 1859; on one side, Neptune; rev. edifice. Fine proof, silver, rare. Size, 22 *Janes*

1632 Same, on tin; pierced.

1633 VALENTINE MOTT, bust; rev. "Awarded To "; by University of New York, medical department. Proof, fair. Size, 22 *Janes*

1634 LOYAL NATIONAL LEAGUE Medal; engraved (for member); "*Dr. H. Spencer, Sacramento, Cal.*" Silver. Size, 23 *Proskey*

1635 COMMITTEE OF VIGILANCE, San Francisco, Cal., 1851; number on schedule, 5949; large eye projecting rays; rev. figure of Justice, standing; thick silver medal of fine quality, and excessively rare; with loop. Size, 24 *Holland*

1636 UNITED BOWMEN of Philadelphia; uninscribed, but intended as a prize medal; head of Appollo; rev. title; and on a schedule, "Field Day." Fine proof, silver. Size, 24

1637 N. Y. STATE VOLUNTEERS; Numismatic and Archæological Soc., Montreal, Canada; Thomas Swan, Mayor of Baltimore; and college medal, Randolph, Macon, Va. Fine medals, on tin. Size, 26. 4 pieces

1638 BENJ. RUSH MEDALS, by *Furst*, 1808, bust; rev. altar, and view of Sydenham; copper. Size, 26. 2 pieces *Janes*

1639 COAST SURVEY; Treasury Department, U. S. A., "For Gallantry and Humanity." Bronze. Size, 22

1640 MAJ. GEN. G. K. WARREN, 1864; rev. Maltese cross; fine proof, tin. Rare. Size, 24 *Janes*

1641 PROF. C. P. BRONSON, A.M., M.D., by his eye patients; copper, by C. C. Wright. Rare. Size, 36 "

1642 ADAM ECKFELDT, chief coiner, U. S. Mint; a farewell tribute from his fellow officers. Copper, by *Furst*. Size, 33

1643 Col. JOHN C. FREMONT, by *Paquet*; rev. "The Rocky Mountains echo back," etc.; fine proof, tin. Scarce. Size, 38 *Haines*

1644 LOUIS KOSSUTH, by *Borrel*, 1854; bust, facing; rev. "ex-Governor of Hungaria set at liberty by the people of the United States of America, 1851." Extremely fine medal; proof, in bronze, scarce. Size, 26 *Anniston*

1645 KOSCIUSZKO, bust; rev. inscription; fine proof, bronze, 1818. Rare. Size, 26

1646 Same; smaller medal, in tin.

1647 GEORGE B. MCCLELLAN. Military bust in high relief; rev. "The Union and the Constitution to be Preserved—No More Arbitrary Arrests—A Cessation of Hostilities and Convention of States, With a View to Peace and Reunion," followed by a long quotation from his report, ~~Splendid medal in bronze. Proof.~~ Electrotype (Rare). Size, 40

1648 Same; bust to l.; rev. "Siege of Yorktown Ended," etc.; ending with Antietam, Sept. 14–17, 1862; laurels and schedule twining below bust of Washington. Fine proof; tin. Size, 33

1649 Same; rev. different inscription, without laurels. Tin, proof. Size, 32

1650 LAFAYETTE; "M. P. I. R. I. G. Motier," etc.; bust to r. encircled by laurel crown, circumscribed by the legend; rev. the General on horseback reviewing the National Guard, Paris, 1789. Extremely fine medal, in bronze. Rare. Size, 33

1651 Same; bust to l.; rev. "Vengeur De La Liberte, dans Des Deux Mondes," etc. Very fine. Rare. Size, 26

1652 Same; bust to r., by *Caunois;* rev. "The Defender of American and French Liberty." Fine medal, in silver. Rare in this metal. Size, 27

1653 Same; impression in copper from same dies.

1654 Another, from slightly different dies.

1655 Same; bust in military dress; rev. "Appelé Par le voeu unanima," etc. 28 Juillet, 1830. Very rare; bronze. Size, 34

1656 Same; rev. "Objet Tour A Tour D'Idolatrie et de la Haine," etc., inscribed in ten parallel lines. Extremely fine; bronze. Scarce. Size, 20

1657 Same; bust of Lafayette; rev. bust of Louis Philippe, done in New York by *Wright & Bale*. Uncirculated. Rare copper. Size, 20

1658 Same; "Lafayette, General-en-Chief," etc., military bust; rev. inscription in parallel lines, circumscribed by HONNEUR ET PATRIE LIBERTE ET ORDRE PUBLIC by by *Pingret*. Very fine and rare; bronze. Size, 17

1659 Same; bust to l. 1789; to r. 1830; rev. ins. on a round tablet; at top, PARIS. Equally fine and rare as last. Same size

1660 Same; others, brass and copper. Fine. 2 pieces

American Medals in various Metals. 79

1661 FRANKLIN; rev. Eropuit Cœlo Fulmen, etc., two varieties. Splendid proof, bronze. Size, 28. 2 pieces

1662 Same; rev. Masonic emblems and inscription, by *Pingret*. Size, 26 — *Hazeltine*

1663 Same; rev. Reward of Merit by the School Committee to (engraved) " A. F. Sears, 1841," by *Stimpson*. Pierced. Extra fine silver medal and rare. Size, 20

1664 Same; head in cap; rev. "Awarded to, etc.," by Franklin Institute, Penn. Bronze proof. Rare. Size, 24

{ 1665 Same; Mechanic Literary Association, Rochester; rev. "Awarded to." Fine proof; bronze. Size, 26

1666 FRANKLIN and Monteyon; rev. ins. Fine proof; bronze. Size, 26

1667 WASHINGTON; Metropolitan Carnival, Feb. 20, 1871, head laureated and encircled by laurel wreath; rev. By Act of Congress, July 16, 1790, The Seat of Government of the United States to be permanently fixed at the City of Washington, etc., e.c.; view of the Capitol. White metal cast. Origin unknown to the writer; possibly unique, certainly very uncommon. A work of merit and value. Size, 48 — *Holland*

1668 Same; Lancaster County Agricultural and Mechanical Society, 1858. Fine proof; copper. Size, 29

1669 Same; Benevolent Society, New York, Liberty crowning bust of Washington, silver. Rare, very good. Size, 26 — *Ahlborn*

1670 Same; rev. "The Hero of Freedom," etc., copper. Fair. Size, 24

1671 Same; rev. "General of the American Armies," etc., by *Twigg*. Tin. Fine. Scarce. Size, 22

1672 Same; by *Wyon*. Tin, proof. Size, 23

1673 Same; Norwalk, Conn., Memorial Medal, 1869; rev. inscription. Fine proof; copper. Size, 25 — *James*

1674 Same medal in tin.

1675 MASONIC; To Commemorate the treaty of 1852; rev. Grand Lodge of Canada, etc. Tin, proof. Size, 26

1676 TEMPERANCE; Medal of the Society founded 1833, by *Halliday*, House of Temperance; in ex. "They shall prosper that love Thee"; rev. Temperance "is the fountain of health;" the pledge on a schedule, coiled like a snake. Fine proof; tin. Rare. Size, 28

1677 Same; rev. pledge in parallel lines. Same size

1678 Same; Temperance is the parent of "Sobriety," "Health," "Industry," "Prudence," etc., etc., on ten schedules, arranged in the form of a plume. Same size — *Holland*

1679 TEMPERANCE; Temperance declaration and pledge, two hands clasped; rev. bust of Washington, by *Lovett*. Same size

1680 Same; from same dies, in brass. Beautiful proof.

1681 Same; The New York Catholic Temperance Association, founded by the Very Rev. Felix Varela, Feb. 9th, 1840; rev. pledge in a cross, pierced. Extremely fine and rare, (so rare as to be generally unknown to collectors). Tin. Size, 28

1682 Same; Catholic Temperance Society, 1841; the pledge below a cross; rev. "Give me this water that I may not thirst," representation of Christ at the well, etc., with key-ring as a loop, by *Mitchell*, *Boston*. Equally fine and rare; tin. Size, 28

1683 Same; Albany Catholic Total Abstinence Association, instituted by Rev. J. A. Schneller, May 3, 1840, by *True*. Proof, tin. Size, 28

1684 Same; the Total Abstinence Society of Ireland, founded by the Very Rev. Father Matthew; rev. representation of Father Matthew administering the pledge; also with key-ring loop. Beautiful proof, tin, same size. Rare.

1685 Same; "Catholic Total Abstinence Society, approved by the Right Rev. John Hughes, D.D."; pledge in a cross. Splendid proof, tin, by *Bale & Smith*. Same size, rare.

1686 Same: medal of the Independent Order of Rechabites; rev. quotation from Luke 1 and 13th. Tin, fine and rare. Size, 24

1687 Same; Herkimer and Montgomery Temperance Society; trefoil in the centre of a circle of 13 stars; rev. pledge. Tin, extremely fine and rare. Size, 22

1688 Same; Certificate of Membership within a wreath of roses; a medal by *Thomas*; man drinking from an old oaken bucket poised on the brink of a well-curb. Only fair, but of great rarity; tin. Size, 23

1689 Same; a medal with a similar obverse, but from another die; the rev. very different. Fine proof, tin, by same; rare. Same size.

1690 Same; Medal by *Bale & Smith*, after Thomas' design of the old oaken bucket, but with a new reverse, for the Young Men's Total Abstinence Society. Fine proof, tin. Size, 24

1691 Same; another, reduced in size, and with an eagle on the reverse. Fine proof.

1692 Same; a series by *Bale*, struck on thick copper planchets; "old oaken bucket"; with different reverses. Size, 22. 3 pieces

American Medals in various Metals. 81

1693 TEMPERANCE. Tin. 3 pieces
1694 Same; Temperance Society, instituted A.D. 1833. Temperance Coat of Arms crested by an Agnus-Dei, "Religion," by *Halliday*. Equally fine and rare; tin. Size, 29
1695 Same; reduced in size. Equally rare, with two others. 3 pieces
1696 RELIGIOUS Medal; centenary offering; representation of "Mrs. Susanna Wesley teaching her son John"; view of Dickinson College. Fine proof, bronze. Size, 26
1697 Same in tin.
1698 Same; child praying; rev. Lord's Prayer, and others; no duplicates. Tin and lead. 7 pieces
1699 ANTI-SLAVERY Society Medal, 1840, by *Bridgens*; "There are more than 2,500,000 slaves in the United States." Fine proof, tin. Size, 30
1700 Same; A voice from Great Britain to America. Tin. Size, 28
1701 ALEXANDER HAMILTON, second Treas. U. S.; fine bust; rev. Edifice, "To Public Credit, 1795." Splendid proof, bronze, by F. Rare. Size, 32
1702 DANIEL WEBSTER, by *C. C. Wright*; bust; rev. column surmounted by a globe. Fine proof, bronze. Size, 50
1703 HENRY CLAY; rev. hand on Constitution; by same; same size. Equally fine.
1704 Duplicate.
1705 JOHN TRUMBULL; Am. Art Union Medal, by same. Bronze, proof. Size, 40
1706 WASHINGTON ALLSTON; same series. Fine proof.
1707 GILBERT STUART; same, slightly rubbed.
1708 WILL PAGE; rev. Pallette; *C. C. Wright*. Fine proof, bronze. Size, 30
1709 JENNY LIND; to commemorate her Charity Concert at Castle Garden, Sept. 11, 1850. Fine proof, bronze. Scarce. Size, 26
1710 EDWARD EVERETT; rev. Penn Institute, incorporated, 1856. Splendid proof, bronze. Size, 28
1711 JOHN PINTARD; rev. New York Hist. Soc.; fine view of the edifice by *Smith & Hartman*; superb medal, in bronze. Rare. Size, 40
1712 WASHINGTON IRVING; rev. Born, etc., Died, etc., in fine wreath of laurel and oak; rare to excess, 18 impressions only having been struck in copper. A splendid proof in this metal. Size, 44
1713 Same, in tin.

1714 CHARLESTOWN (Mass.); Centennial Antique Association, 1875; rev. a "two-minute man" a comical affair in tin, on thick planchet.　Size, 40

1715 ODD FELLOWS Hall; a rare old medal, with a view of the edifice. Proof, tin.　Size, 24

1716 DAVID HOSACK, by *Furst;* rev. "Arts and Science." Fine proof, bronze.　Size, 22

1717 STONEWALL JACKSON, tin; proof, by *Caque.*

1718 Medal struck to commemorate "the return of peace," (in Europe). 1871. Fine proof, in copper, brass, and tin. Size, 18.　3 pieces

1719 DR. E. K. KANE; to commemorate his birth, Arctic expedition, and death; copper. Rare.　Size, 24

[The following medals, twelve in number, are of great and increasing interest to American numismatists and archæologists. They are directly historical and free from the vague allusions and applications than render so many of our early medals unsatisfactory].

1720 LOUIS XIV., bust to r.; rev. America seated on a rock, supporting the French shield; COLONIA FR. STABILITA; and in ex. "Angl. ex. insula St. Christop. exturbat, 1666." Fine proof, bronze; very rare.
　Size, 26

1721 Same; bust to r.; rev. France seated on a rock under pine trees; flags, a beaver, and river god near: FRANCIA IN NOVO ORBE VICTRIX; in ex. "Kebeca Liberata, 1690"; fine proof, bronze. Very rare.　Size, 26

[This medal was struck to commemorate the failure of the expedition led by Sir William Phipps against Quebec, which was defended by the French Count de Frontenac. It was essentially a New England enterprise, having for its object the punishment of the French Canadians for the destruction of Salmon Falls, Kuskebé, and other towns just previously].

1722 GEO. II.; bust to l.; rev. a shield, bearing an inverted Fleur-de-lis, circumscribed PERFIDA EVERSA; unicorn and lion to r. and l., etc., etc.; yellow bronze. Extremely fine, rare.　Size, 26

1723 Same; obv. like last; rev. Britannia in a car drawn by a lion, her attendants, Liberty and Justice; the ground under their feet strewn with Fleur-de-lis; FŒDVS INVECTVM, etc., etc. Equally fine and rare; a companion medal.

1724 Another of the same series, with the reverses of the last two medals for obverse and reverse. Same condition and value.

1725 Duplicate, equally fine.

1726 Another; obv. a globe with soldier and sailor pointing to "Canada" above, Fame blowing a trumpet; under-

neath, France prostrate; rev. "Louisbourg taken 1758"; view of the attack. Fine proof, bronze; rare.
Size, 28

GEO. II.; equally or nearly as fine.

One with Britannia standing, one foot resting on a prow, in her right hand a trident, in her left a standard surmounted by a lion; MOORE BARRINGTON; in ex. "Soc. Prom. Arts and Commerce"; rev. GAUDALUPE SURRENDERS; in ex. "May 1, 1759"; fine proof, bronze. Very rare.
Size, 25

GEORGE II., bust; rev. female under a pine tree, sitting on the ground weeping; CANADA SUBDUED, 1760; fine proof, bronze. Very rare.
Size, 25

LOUIS XVIII., bust; rev. GALLIA ET AMERICA FOEDERATA; figures emblematical of the two countries standing beside a pillar surmounted by a caryotid bust of Mercury or Hermes; fine proof, bronze. Rare.
Size, 32

Another, on planchet of double thickness. Very rare.

United States Cents.

1793. Head, hair flowing; rev. endless chain, in legend AMERI.; obv. fine; rev. *very* fine. Rare.

Another of this rare type, very sharp; has been cleaned.

Same date and type, but "United States of AMERICA" around the chain; extremely fine, barely circulated. Very valuable and rare.

Another, same type; a variety of the chain cent, with close date and no dot after the word "Liberty." *Fine* and rare.

One *with* the dot, quite a different head, but little circulated, but rather weak obverse, and scratched; the reverse stronger and finer. Very rare.

Same date; rev. "One Cent," within olive wreath; a splendid uncirculated cent, with fine steel color and polished surface, without the slightest scratch or abrasion, only the tips of the masses of hair touched by friction. Rare and valuable.

Another of this type, the obverse from the same die; the reverse from a different die, the sprigs of berries in the wreath much shorter; *almost* as fine as last; a superb and valuable cent.

A cent of this date, never in circulation, with ONE HUNDRED FOR A DOLLAR impressed on the edge; the planchet before receiving the impression was a little rough and the lines were not all removed by the

1740 One with the ordinary ornamentation on the edge, the trefoil between the head and date more broad and spreading than on other varieties; the obv. die appearing to have *sprung* across the centre. *Extremely fine;* rare.

1741 One, and the last of this type, considerably rubbed across the masses of hair, but in all respects a good cent.

1742 Same date, on a broader planchet, with a Liberty cap on a pole over the shoulder; from the sound dies. Extremely fine and rare.

1743 Another of the "Liberty cap" type. Fine impression, but the surface behind the head hurt by corrosion; still *very* fine for the type.

1744 1794; on a broad planchet resembling the cents of the previous year. Rare variety and extremely fine.

1745 One on a smaller and thicker planchet, with high milled rim. Very fine.

1746 A cent of this date, with ONE HUNDRED A DOLLAR (the FOR omitted) on the edge. In only fair condition, but excessively rare.

1747 A sequence of seven varieties of the cents of this date. Every one fine. 7 pieces

1748 1795; on thick planchet, the lettering continued on the edge. Fine; rare variety.

1749 Another, equally fine; the lettering on the edge continued, but the planchet thinner. Rare.

1750 One with the edge plain; on the obverse a broader milling, "one cent" higher within the wreath on the reverse; almost a proof impression, but *slightly* circulated. Rare.

1751 One equally fine; ONE CENT in the centre of the wreath. Very desirable.

1752 A strictly uncirculated cent of this date and type; on thick planchet, but with the edge plain. Very rare.

1753 A variety known as the "Jefferson head"; a very fair impression. Excessively rare.

1754 A duplicate of this rare variety. Rather poor.

1755 1796; Liberty cap behind the head. Fine, but little circulated. Rare.

1756 Same, marked by Mr. Brevoort No. 3 obverse, No. 2 reverse; on a planchet of unusual thickness, resembling one variety of the preceding year; dark, but sharp. Very rare.

United States Cents.

One of this date, with a ribbon or "fillet" around the head; red and uncirculated. Very rare. — Ahlborn
Another, with broad milling, on thick planchet; a slight crack on the obv. die. Uncirculated, and *excessively rare*. — Merritt
1797; a beautiful uncirculated nearly proof impression; fine red color. Very rare. — Windsor
Another equally fine; a slight difference in the wreath on reverse; rounder leaves. — Hazeltine
Duplicate of No. 1759; splendid example. Fine red color. — Ahlborn
1798; with slight milling around the rim, hardly perceptible. *Extremely* fine; rare. — Smith
Another, with narrow milling, but a distinct variety; the rim raised. Very fine. — Merritt
One with broad milling on both sides, from the die 1797. A fine example and rare. — "
1799; fine impression, not much circulated; the surface a little rough, but altogether an uncommonly desirable cent. Very rare. — Rugg
Another, very fine for this date; would by some be preferred to the first. — "
1800; uncirculated, good color. In this condition very rare. — Ahlborn
Others, varieties. Very good. 2 pieces — Frossard
1801; extremely fine. Nearly uncirculated. — Hazeltine
Same; two varieties. Very fine. 2 pieces — Merritt
Others of this date; variety. Very good. 3 pieces — Hazeltine
1802; uncirculated, light olive. Rare. — "
Same, from broken die; uncirculated, steel color. Very desirable. — Ahlborn
One from same die; bright, nearly proof surface; a superb cent, but may have been cleaned. — Hazeltine
One from perfect die, companion to last. Equally fine. — Haines
1803; an uncirculated cent; original color; that part of the surface not red a beautiful light olive. Very rare in this condition. — Ahlborn
A variety of this date. Uncirculated. — "
Another variety; larger date and letters; cracked die. Extremely fine. — Smith
1804; an extremely fine impression from the perfect die; has rarely been equalled at a public sale. Very rare. — Rugg
Another slight variety, unusually fine for date. — Hazeltine
1805; fine uncirculated cent; olive color, with traces of red. Very rare and desirable. — Merritt
Another. Fine. — Bryant

United States Cents.

1783 1806; a perfect match for No. 1781 in color, and nearly uncirculated; there are few cents of this date of the quality of this. Very rare.
1784 Another variety, nearly as fine. Rare.
1785 1807; from the die of 1806; both dates apparent. Extremely fine.
1786 Another, same variety; equally fine or finer, but of a greenish tint. Very rare.
1787 1808; extremely fine, almost uncirculated. Rare in this condition.
1788 Another; same description; hardly inferior.
1789 1809; a beautiful and nearly uncirculated example; fine in every quality, color, preservation, and impression. Very rare.
1790 Another; fine for date and variety. Very rare.
1791 1810; uncirculated, splendid impression. Very rare.
1792 One of this date from the dies of 1809. Very fine; rare.
1793 Same, both varieties. Fine. 2 pieces
1794 1811; very sharp and fine; has been cleaned.
1795 One from the dies of 1810. Very fine.
1796 1812; a beautiful uncirculated cent; almost a proof impression; has been cleaned; still highly desirable.
1797 One equally fine; olive color.
1798 1813; extremely fine; steel color. Rare.
1799 One equally fine; olive color. Very rare.
1800 1814; extremely fine; beautiful color and polish; probably has been cleaned.
1801 Same; the figure 4 in date without crosslet; uncirculated, dark. Rare.
1802 Another; double chin; uncirculated, but tarnished.
1803 1816; perfect die; uncirculated. Scarce.
1804 Same; broken die. Red, and uncirculated.
1805 1817; high milled rim; splendid impression; fine original red. Rare.
1806 Duplicate; fine olive color.
1807 Same date; low rim; a distinct variety; red, and uncirculated.
1808 A variety with 15 stars around the head of Liberty; steel color, uncirculated. Rare.
1809 Duplicate of this variety, equally fine.
1810 1818; perfect die; uncirculated; red.
1811 Same; crack in die between stars; uncirculated.
1812 Same; with head of 1817. Ex. fine.
1813 1819; high rim and strongly *dentilated* milling. A beautiful uncirculated impression and rare variety.

United States Cents.

1819; different milling and smaller date; red and uncirculated.

Another duplicate, equally fine.

Others; distinct varieties; strictly uncirculated. 2 pieces

1820; perfect die; high rim and milling; splendid uncirculated impression. Very rare.

Same; cracked die; line connecting stars. Red and uncirculated.

Another; violet color; proof polish.

Others like No. 1818 and 1819; brilliant. 2 pieces

1821; uncirculated; proof polish; steel color; slight marks of friction. Rare.

Same; a variety. Equally fine.

Others; variety; olive color; very fine. 2 pieces

1822; beautiful *proof* impression; as such very rare.

Same; uncirculated and red. Rare.

One with a line inside the milling on the left half of the obverse; splendid uncirculated impression. Very rare.

1823; fine *proof* impression from the die of 1822; beautiful color and entirely without scratch or stain. Rare to excess.

Same; uncirculated; red still remaining on reverse; obv. a little rough, but altogether a beautiful cent. Rare.

One of this date from broken die. Unusually fine and sharp, but with scratches. Rare.

Cent of this date restruck. Brilliant.

Duplicate of last.

1824; extremely fine; hardly circulated; fine steel color. Rare.

Same date; distinct variety. Good.

1825; beautiful and strictly uncirculated; original color. Very rare.

Another uncirculated cent of this date; reverse different. Very rare.

1826; uncirculated; fine olive color.

Same; different die; line inside the milling, and small break in the die; nearly uncirculated. Rare.

Another, with larger break in die; strictly uncirculated. Very rare.

1827; uncirculated; every star sharp, which is seldom the case. Rare.

Same; weaker impression from another die; fine olive color. Very fine.

United States Cents.

1841 1828 ; Fine proof impression ; steel color, without a scratch. Rare.

1842 Same ; nearly uncirculated cent of a light olive color. Fine and rare.

1843 Duplicate ; equally fine.

1844 1829 ; uncirculated ; strong impression ; fine steel color. Rare.

1845 Same ; a variety ; a line connecting the stars to left of Liberty head. Very fine.

1846 Others ; varieties. Very fine.

1847 1830 ; uncirculated, but stars not sharp and pointed ; olive color. Scarce.

1848 Same ; distinct varieties. Very fine. 2 pieces

1849 1831 ; uncirculated ; bright. Rare.

1850 Others, nearly as fine, varieties. 2 pieces

1851 1832 ; uncirculated, but the stars a little dull ; olive color. Scarce.

1852 Same ; a variety. Fine.

1853 1833 ; uncirculated and bright on obverse ; rev. olive color. Desirable.

1854 Another and stronger impression ; every star perfect ; fine color throughout and strictly uncirculated. Rare.

1855 Others ; varieties. All very fine. 3 pieces

1856 1834 ; uncirculated ; almost proof. Rare.

1857 Same, from the die with " double face." Very fine.

1858 1835 ; strong uncirculated, nearly proof cent, fine steel color inclining to red. Rare.

1859 Another of this date from broken die ; very fine. Nearly uncirculated.

1860 Duplicate of the first of this date and equally fine. Rare.

1861 1836 ; uncirculated ; fine olive color ; slight break in obverse die. Scarce.

1862 Others ; two varieties. Very fine. 2 pieces

1863 1837 ; uncirculated ; bright red. Scarce.

1864 Same ; slight variety. Equally fine.

1865 1838. Red and uncirculated ; every star pointed, which is rarely the case, even when bright. Rare.

1866 Same date ; beautiful impression and color. Also uncirculated.

1867 1839 ; head of " '38." Extremely fine.

1868 Same ; new head, lock on brow. Equally fine.

1869 Booby head ; strictly uncirculated. Rare.

1870 With head of 1840. Very fine.

1871 Set of the four varieties, as described. All fine.

United States Half Cents. 89

1872 1840. Uncirculated and red. A beautiful and rare cent; small date.
1873 Same; large date. Rare.
1874 Both varieties. Fine. 2 pieces
1875 1841. Fine.
1876 1842. Uncirculated, original, red color. Rare.
1877 Same; large and small dates. Very fine. 2 pieces
1878 1843. Red and uncirculated. Scarce.
1879 Same; large date. Equally fine.
1880 Both varieties. Uncirculated. 2 pieces
1881 1844. Uncirculated, red. Scarce.
1882 Others. Very fine. 2 pieces
1883 1845. Uncirculated. Scarce.
1884 Same variety. Equally fine.
1885 1846. Uncirculated; bright.
1886 Same. Uncirculated; bronzed.
1887 1847. Uncirculated; bright.
1888 1848. Uncirculated; red.
1889 Same; bright; slight stain.
1890 1849. Uncirculated; red.
1891 1850. Uncirculated; bright.
1892 1851. Uncirculated; almost proof and brilliant.
1893 1852. Same.
1894 1853. Same.
1895 1854. Same.
1896 1855. Same.
1897 Same; oblique date. Proof. Rare.
1898 1856. Uncirculated; bright.
1899 1857. Large and small date, bright. 2 pieces.
1900 Same; large date, tarnished proof.
1901 1846 to 1857 inclusive. All bright and uncirculated. 14 pieces
1902 Nickel cents, '57, '8, '9, '60-'2 and '3; all brilliant. Several proofs. 6 pieces
1903 Copper; two cents of 1864, '5, '6, '7, '8, '9, and '70; all brilliant proofs. 7 pieces

HALF CENTS.

1904 1793. Uncirculated, but stained and slightly corroded. Rare.
1905 Another; very fine, but little circulated. Rare.
1906 1794. Extremely fine, rare.
1907 1795. A beautiful uncirculated coin, *as it fell from the die*, and the rare variety, "Two hundred for a dollar," on the edge. Very rare.
1908 One with plain edge and broad milling; the planchet size, 16 (a full size larger than last); so far as known to writer, unique; faint impression, but little worn.
1909 Same on smaller planchet, narrower milling; the piece not a full circle; nearly uncirculated. Rare.

1910 Duplicate of the variety first described (1907). Very fine, rare.
1911 1796. Brilliant impression, from Dr. Edwards' dies. Very rare.
1912 1797. Extremely fine, barely circulated. Rare.
1913 1800. Uncirculated; red. Very rare.
1914 1802. From die of 1800; very fine, in fine condition. Very rare.
1915 1803. Very fine.
1916 1804. Uncirculated. Rare in this condition.
1917 1805. Red and uncirculated.
1918 1806. In the same beautiful condition.
1919 1807 and '8. Very fine. 2 pieces
1920 1809. Uncirculated.
1921 1809 and '10. Fine. 2 pieces
1922 1811. Very fine, rare.
1923 Same restruck; brilliant. Rare.
1924 1825 and 1826. Very fine. 2 pieces
1925 1828. A beautiful uncirculated piece; red, with proof polish. Very rare.
1926 Same; strictly uncirculated, red.
1927 1829. Uncirculated; red, proof polish. Rare.
1928 Same; light olive.
1929 1832 and 1833. Very fine. 2 pieces
1930 1833. Brilliant proof; very rare.
1931 1833 and 1834. Very fine. 2 pieces
1932 1834. Brilliant proof, rare.
1933 1835. Uncirculated.
1934 1837. "Half cent worth pure copper," uncirculated.
1935 1841. Old tarnished proof. Very rare.
1936 1847. Brilliant Proof. Very rare.
1937 1848. Same. Rare.
1938 1849. Small date, same. Rare.
1939 Same; small date, with 1850, both uncirculated. 2 pieces
1940 1851. Proof, red.
1941 1852. Brilliant proof. Very rare.
1942 1853 and 1854. Both uncirculated. 2 pieces
1943 1855, '6, and '7. Uncirculated, brilliant. 3 pieces
1944 1857. Brilliant proof. Rare.

Trial-Pieces, Patterns, Etc.

1945 1776. CONTINENTAL CURENCY (sic); fine proofs from dies intended for coining dollars (?) Tin, scarce.
1946 1790. Standish Barry threepence, or "Baltimore Town" piece; pierced and plugged, otherwise good. Very rare.
1947 1790. CHURCH PENNY; a rare token used at Albany at this date. See Mickley Catalogue, 2471. Valuable.

Trial-Pieces, Patterns, Etc.

1948 1792. Trial-piece designed for U. S. cent; eagle on half shield. Rare.
1949 KENTUCKY Cent; a halfpenny struck in England about 1796? Extremely fine, scarce.
1950 1822; trial from obv. die for Half-Dollar, in copper. Proof, unique.
1951 1836; Gold Dollar, liberty cap and rays; rev. value, etc. Proof, rare.
1952 1836; first Steam Coinage, Feb. 22. Fine, very scarce.
1953 Same; struck March 23. Fine proof.
1954 1837; Feuchtwanger's composition, "Three Cents"; rev. Arms of New York. Uncirculated.
1955 Same; rev. Eagle standing with raised wings on a rock. Original, uncirculated, very rare.
1956 Same date; "One Cent"; same composition. Uncirculated. Two varieties. 2 pieces
1957 1838; Half-dollar, head of Liberty draped in the Roman manner, diadem on brow, and ribbon with "Liberty" thereon; around, thirteen stars; reverse, eagle displayed, arrows and olive-branch in his talons. Splendid proof, and rare to excess.
1958 1838; same; obverse like last; reverse, eagle flying to left; crack in the die. Splendid proof, equally rare.
1960 1850; "Cent, one-tenth silver." Rare.
1961 1851; "I Cent;" reverse, Liberty seated. Proof in copper, rare.
1962 1852; Gold ring Dollar; "United States of America," and date. Rare.
1963 1853; One Cent; Liberty head. Pure nickel, rare.
1964 1854; One Cent; Liberty head. Copper.
1965 1855; One Cent; flying eagle. Pure nickel, very rare.
1966 NICKEL Cent, without date; type of '56. Very fine and rare.
1967 1858; One Cent, in nickel. Indian head.
1968 1858; same in copper. Splendid proof, very rare.
1969 1858; nickel pattern-cent; struck in copper. Rare.
1970 1859; Half-Dollars; set of five patterns in silver; on four, French head of Liberty, with different reverses; on one, Liberty seated; reverse, eagle displayed. All brilliant proofs; as a set, rare. 5 pieces
1971 1859; Half-dollar in copper, like the last one of No. 1970, with two varieties of the head of Liberty.
3 pieces
1972 1859; Double Eagle ($20), struck in copper. Rare.

3 ¢ 1973 1861; annual assay; "Mint of the United States."
         Fine proof, bronze.   Size, 21
2 5 1974 1861; Twenty Dollars; Clark, Gruber & Co., Denver.
         Proof in copper, with milled edge.
5 ¢ 1975 1861; set of Clark, Gruber & Co.'s gold coins, viz.,
         Double-Eagle, Eagle, Half-Eagle, and Quarter ditto,
         with *plain edges*. Struck in copper, brilliant proofs,
         very rare.   4 pieces
3 0 1976 1862; Ten d., "God our Trust," on schedule; and
         companion, "God our Trust," in field. Copper.
                                                          2 pieces
5 5¢ 1977 1863; large 3 Cents; obverse, head of Liberty; re-
         verse, "United States of America." Splendid proof.
         Copper.   Size, 18
5 5 1978 1863; 2 Cents; "God and Our Country"; head of
         Washington. Splendid proof in nickel.
× 1 1979 1863; same; splendid proof in copper.
2 5 1980 1863; same; shield instead of head of Washington.
         Nickel.
6 5 1981 1863; Half-Dollar; motto on schedule, "God Our
         Trust." Fine proof.
6 0 1982 1863; same, with motto in field.
3 5 1983 1864; Three cents (*sic*); rev. eagle with a copperhead in
         his talons; Feuchtwanger's composition. Scarce.
2 0 1984 1865; 3 dollars, struck in nickel.
/ / 1985 1865; III. (cents), struck in copper.
1 7 5 1986 1866; 5 cents, "In God we trust;" bust of Washington;
         nickel. Proof; rare.
         1987 1866; same; motto over shield; nickel.
         1988 1866; same; divided date, same type; nickel.
2 0 0 1989 1867; Longacre's beautiful pattern, 5 cents; struck in
         aluminum. Brilliant proof; rare.
2 5 1990 1867; other patterns of this date, 5 cents.   2 pieces
/ 7 5 1991 1867; annual assay, " Mint of the United States";
         Silver nickel. Rare.   Size, 21
3 0 1992 1868; 5 cents, head of Liberty; reverse, large V; nickel.
         Silver Rare.
/ 0 0 1993 1869; annual assay, "Let us have peace," Liberty
         seated; struck in nickel. Rare.   Size, 21

Foreign Medals in Different Metals.

  1994 Silver medal of Cornelius and John De Witt, brothers,
         killed by a mob in 1671, their busts vis-a-vis; rev. the
         mob represented as wild beasts, killing them; a shell
         medal of the period mentioned, the field burnished.
         Very fine and rare.   Size, 46
         [From the collection of Hon. Charles Furman, Charleston, S. C.]

Foreign Medals in Different Metals. 93

1995 SYDENHAM Crystal Palace, by *Dowler* of Birmingham; view of the palace; tin. Size, 46

1996 TIN medal of Joseph Priestly, the Philosopher, by *Phipson*. Proof. Size, 34

1997 DANIEL O'CONNELL, Esq., M. P., bust, full face; rev. born 6 Aug., 1775, died 15 May, 1847; proof in tin. Very rare. Size, 29

1998 SCHILLER and six other white medals. 8 pieces

1999 LOUIS XVI.; rev. ABANDON DE TOUS LES PRIVILEGES; picture of a scene in the French Parliament; medal of the Hon. Wm. Pitt; of the Cathedral de Chartres; of Charles X., Rex Christianissimus, etc.; large bronze. Very fine. 6 pieces

2000 MEDALS of the British Archæological Association; very beautiful; no duplicate; bronze. Size, 22. 4 pieces

2001 ANNE, Queen of England, on the capture of Barcelona, 1706, bronze; St. Hilaire and Caroline of Brunswick (without reverse), and others, tin and plated. 5 pieces

2002 CAROLUS LINNÆUS, with his 24 classes of plants, a typical example of each kind; fine proof. Very scarce; tin. Size, 30

2003 Same, from series Numismatica. Fine proof; bronze. Size, 26

2004 BENJ. WEST, inscribed to his memory by G. Mills, Franklin and Montyon, James Watts, etc. All very fine medals; bronze. 4 pieces

2005 CAPT. COOK, J. Lelewel (numismatist), Linnæus, F. Henry Egerton, and seven others. All bronze; different sizes. 12 pieces
[A valuable lot.]

2006 NICOLAS POUSSIN, Alex. Pirou, Girondet, and four medals of exquisite workmanship for reward of merit, by such artists as *Denou* and *Tiolier*. About size 26; all bronze. 7 pieces

2007 MEDALS of the Galerie Metallique, Numismatica and other series. All bronze and fine proof impressions. 12 pieces

2008 GOETHE, by *Bovy;* rev. Ianus head, above eagle, below lion. *Extremely* fine work; bronze. Size, 26
[All the remaining medals under this head are bronze, and the immediately succeeding lots of extraordinary excellence.]

2009 HENRY II. and Katherine de Medecis, busts of both (on opposite sides) to the waist, under the latter 1555. Superb proof. Size, 38

2010 Exact duplicate.

2011 HENRY II. alone, bust as before; rev. OBRES IN ITAL

94   *Foreign Medals in Different Metals.*

GERM ET GAL FORTITER GESTAS, three symbolical figures on a car drawn by four horses. Splendid proof.

2012 LEOPOLD I., bust; rev. "Pace populorum," etc., stork descending with civic crown, 1706. Fine proof.
Size, 36

2013 DUCHESS DE BARRY and Marie Terrese, Mademoiselle, 1827; busts on opposite sides by *Puymaurin* and *Dubois*. Beautiful proof.   Size, 32

2014 LUD·MAGNUS FR. ET NAV REX, bust royally draped; rev. MAIESTATI ÆTERNIT, etc., grand edifice. Splendid proof.   Size, 32

2015 Equally fine, but different medal of like character.
Size, 32

2016 REMBRANDT; obv. "REMBRANDT HERMANSZ, VAN RYN NE A LEYDEN, 15 JUILLET 1606 MORT A AMSTERDAM ET ENTERRE 8 OCT., 1668," bust in cap and lace collar; rev. a representation of his great painting, "La Ronde de Nuit." A medal as remarkable for its excellence as magnitude.   Size, 75

2017 ALBERT EDWARD, Prince of Wales; bust by *Wyon*; rev. his crest. Magnificent.   Size, 36

2018 HENRY DE LOR, Duc de Guise, bust; rev. "Pax Nubila Terris." Beautiful proof; old work of quality. Size, 52

2019 LEIBNITZ. By Academy of Prussia. 1846. Fine proof.
Size, 34

2020 GUSTAVUS III. Sweden. By *Kuchler*. Bust royally draped; rev. tomb, etc. Very splendid proof. Size, 36

2021 H. VERNET. By the Academy of Fine Arts, France. View of the edifice. Fine proof.   Size, 30

2022 HENRY III. Bust; rev. "Duo Protego Unit;" 1598; two sceptres and sword crossed and palmated. Beautiful proof.   Size, 28

2023 MEDAL in Honor of Charles James Fox. Bust nearly full face. In two half circles, "Glory to the intrepid Fox—Firm as old Albion's battered rocks;" rev. ins. edge lettered. Thick, penny size. Red and uncirculated. Very rare.

2024 MEDAL or placque, nearly diamond shape. Ends square (probably French revolutionary). Large eye within wreath on a garnished fasces, with ax; rev. plain.   22x46

2025 Two fine medals, by *Looz*. Ins. in German. On one, the sun shining on a rock which stands in the sea; on the other, an angel with crown and harp.   Size, 24
2 pieces

2026 Another, more elaborate, in honor of an old Margrave,

of Brandenburg, Ludwig by name. 1324–1361. Beautiful reverse. One of the finest pieces of medallic work that we have seen. Size, 33
A LARGE Medal, struck to commemorate the union of Cologne and Anvers, by Radway. 1843. Anchor, on which hang two shields; rev. two river gods, "Escaut—Rhin." By *Hart*. Extremely fine.
Size, 48
THE Duke d'Orleans. By same artist. Bust; rev. Belgium standing by a tomb; in ex." Chambres Legislatives De Belgique," etc. Same size as last.
Another Medal, by same, in honor of J. B. Cluysennar, architect. Size, 44
LOUIS XVI., Louis XVII., and Louis XVIII. All extremely fine and historic medals. Size, 32. 3 pieces
GEORGE CUVIER. Long ins. on rev. Beautiful proof.
Size, 32
JOS–LOU–LAGRANGE and G. L. Giesecke; rev. Arctic scene, and another. All proofs. 3 pieces
THORWALDSEN, and three others. All proofs. 4 pieces
BLUCHER (Von Walstatt). Bust; rev. Victory going before a Quadriga driven by Blucher, a thunderbolt in his right hand. Splendid medal. Size, 26
ISAAC NEWTON. Series Numismatica.
MARTIN LUTHER. Bust; rev. "The Third Jubilee of the Reformation Celebrated at Paris," etc. Fine proof. Rare. Size, 26

[ALL THAT FOLLOW ARE FRENCH.]

HENRY I., 1070–1135. Henry II., 1133–1182.
2 pieces
LOUIS XIV.; rev. "Incensa Batavorum." Fine proof.
Size, 26
Same; rev. two busts vis-a-vis, Lud. and Adelaide. Beautiful proof. Same size
LOUIS XV. Different reverses. Same size. 2 pieces
ST. HÉLÈNE medal, in honor of General Gourgaud and others. All extra fine. Av. size, 26. 10 pieces
MEDALET of Napoleon 1st, struck in 1796, when he was General-in-Chief. Loop removed, youthful bust, long hair; rev. Minerva seated. Copper gilt. *Extremely* fine and rare. Size, 22
Same as First Consul, by *Andrieu*; rev. Paix DE LUNEVILLE. Rare. Size, 27
Another on same occasion, but from a different die.
Another as First Consul; bust above a tablet and flags; rev. Passage Dec. 9th, St. Bernard, etc. Fine proof, rare. Size, 38

2046 NAPOLEON, Emperor; rev. sojourn at Elba; beautiful proof by *Brenet*. Rare. Size, 26
2047 Same; Emperor and King; rev. rays proceeding from an eagle, between the lines, the names of battle-fields. Fine proof. Size, 32
2048 Same; rev. "L'Exile Abregea Les Jours"; View of St. Helena, by *Borrel*. Size, 32
2049 Medal to commemorate the conquest of Egypt; Sphinx head; rev. crocodile chained to a palm tree. Fine proof. Size, 22
2050 TO THE ARMY OF ITALY; rev. Hercules slaying a monster with 7 heads. Size, 28
2051 MONERON Cinq-Sols; rev. Hercules wasting his muscle on a bundle of rods; beautiful proof. Rare. Size, 25
2052 Same; representation of soldiers in an incuse, oval cartouche; beautiful proof. Rare as such.
2053 DEUX Sols; rev. Liberty seated, with medalets of historical interest, struck at the same time. All uncirculated and scarce. 4 pieces
2054 OCTAGONAL Medal of "Conseil Des Cinq-Cents"; a snake ring around the "Constitution De L'an Trois"; rev. cap of Liberty on a fasces. Beautiful proof. Size, 28x26
2055 Medals of the "CONSEIL DES ANCIENS," and "COMMISSARIES CIVILS." Rare. Size, 24. 2 pieces
2056 PRISE de la Bastille, 1789; rev. "Le Donjon de Vincenne, 1844," by *Rogat*. Fine proof. Size, 28
2057 L. PHILIPPE accepting the crown in 1830, his bust guarded by a lion; rev. "LIBERTE ORDRE PUBLIC." Size, 38
2058 MEDAL of the Commune of 1792, "Exemple Aux Peuple," Liberty making a chowder of the imperial trappings. Beautiful proof; rare. Size, 36
2059 OVAL medal by *Du Vivier*, of the "Council D'Etat" of the old Republic. Beautiful proof; rare. Size, 30x24
2060 PICTURE of the siege of the Bastile, 1789; rev. Nemesis, 1789–1830 27th July, 1840. Fine proof. Size, 26
2061 RETURN of the Emperor from Elba, 1815. Splendid proof by *Denon*. Rare. Size, 26
2062 SERIES of fine, valuable, and rare medals of the Revolution of 1830. Size, 24. 4 pieces
2063 Others, smaller; very thick, of superior work. Size, 18 4 pieces
2064 Similar medals, inspired by the arrival of the Emperor's remains from St. Helena, in 1840, and on other occasions; all relating to Napoleon I. 3 pieces

2065 NATIONAL SOUVERAINETI, 1789-1848, with a fine head of Liberty; in copper and tin; rare. Size, 24. 2 pieces

2066 "LA SUITE PROCHAINEMENT"; four french ragamuffins kicking each other as they march in single file: on the other side, inscription; a curious and rare medal, with two others, large and small. 3 pieces

2067 NAPOLEON III.; a beautiful medal by *Borrel*; to commemorate his coronation by "Universal Suffrage," the number of votes, 7-824-189, recorded on a tablet; mounted in a brass rim, gilt. Size of all, 38. *Rare*.

2068 CHARLES Lucien Jules Lawrence Bonaparte; bust; rev. record of his birth and death, "Les Amis de la Science." Beautiful medal by *Dumont & Pouscarme*. Size, 32

2069 MEDAL of Charles Philippi, brother of Louis Philippi. Fine proof. Same size as last

2070 A series of medals, executed under the direction of *Puymaurin*, illustrative of the reign of Louis XVIII. The heads are uniform; engraved by *Andrieu*; the reverses as various as the number of medals. Exceptionally fine as to quality and condition. Size, 32 28 pieces

2071 A series of smaller medals of the same King; by same. 7 pieces

2072 Similar series of Charles X., by *Depaulis & Puymaurin*. Size, 32. 10 pieces

2073 Others, with two of Napoleon III. 5 pieces

National Medals.

[All in fine order and proof.]

PRESIDENTIAL, BRONZE.

2074 JOHN ADAMS; bust; rev. tomahawk and pipe crossed above two clasped hands, PEACE AND FRIENDSHIP. Size, 32

2075 Duplicate.

2076 JAMES MADISON, 1809; large olive bronze medal, same type; scarce. Size, 48

2077 Same; reduced in size; red bronze. Size, 40

2078 JAMES MONROE, 1817; same; olive bronze. Size, 48

2079 Same; reduced; red bronze. Size, 40

2080 JOHN QUINCY ADAMS, 1825; same as last. Size, 40

2081 Same; bust draped in the Roman style; below, "March 4, 1825"; rev. Minerva extending an olive branch to America; SCIENCE GIVES PEACE AND AMERICA PLENTY. Fine proof in dark tin. *Very rare*. Size, 32

National Medals.

2082 ANDREW JACKSON, 1829; bust; rev. pipe and hatchet crossed and hands clasped; olive bronze; rare.
Size, 48

2083 Same; reduced in size; red bronze. Size, 40

2084 MARTIN VAN BUREN, 1837; same; olive bronze. Size, 48

2085 Same; smaller; red olive bronze. Size, 40

2086 Duplicate; same size.

2087 JOHN TYLER, 1841; same; olive bronze. Size, 48

2088 Same; reduced; red bronze. Size, 40

2089 JAMES K. POLK, 1845; same; olive bronze. Size, 48

2090 Same; reduced; red bronze. Size, 40

2091 ZACHARY TAYLOR, 1849; Same; olive bronze. Size, 48

2092 JAMES BUCHANAN, 1857; bust; rev. "To Dr. Frederick Rose, Asst. Surgeon Royal Navy, G. B., for kindness and humanity to officers and crew of U. S. Steamer Susquehanna." Æsculapius rescuing victims from Time. Size, 48

2093 Same; rev. In Commemoration of the first Embassy from Japan, 1860. Size, 48

2094 Duplicate.

2095 Same; bust, front face; rev. "THE UNION MUST AND SHALL BE PRESERVED," struck in yellow brass; rare. Size, 40

2096 ANDREW JOHNSON, 1865; bust; rev. within branches of oak and olive tied with a ribbon, "WITH COURAGE AND FIDELITY HE DEFENDED," etc.; red bronze.
Size, 48

2097 GEN. U. S. GRANT, 1869; rev. "I INTEND TO FIGHT IT OUT ON THIS LINE IF IT TAKES ALL SUMMER," etc.
Size, 38

2098 Same; rev. Inaugurated, etc.; tin. Size, 32

2099 Same; "The oceans united by railway May 10, 1868"; rev. rocky mountain scene, train of cars passing.
Size, 30

ARMY.

2100 MAJ.-GEN. GATES; on the surrender of Gen. Burgoyne, at Saratoga, Oct. 17, 1777. An exquisite piece of work by *N. Gatteaux*. Size, 34

2101 Same, in tin.

2102 GEN. DANIEL MORGAN; on the victory at Cowpens, Mar. 9, 1781, by *Dupré*. Size, 36

2103 Duplicate.

2104 COL. JOHN EDGAR HOWARD; for intrepidity at the same battle (Cowpens). *Du Vivier*. Size, 30

2105 Duplicate.

National Medals. 99

2106 COL. WILLIAM WASHINGTON; in honor of the same battle, by *Du Vivier*. Size, 30
2107 Duplicate.
2108 COL. GEORGE CROGHAN; for his gallant defence of Fort Stephenson on Sandusky Bay, Aug. 2, 1813, by *Furst*. Size, 40
2109 MAJ.-GEN. WILLIAM H. HARRISON; for the victory of the Thames, Oct. 5, 1813, by *Furst*. Size, 40
2110 MAJ.-GEN. WINFIELD SCOTT; for distinguished services in the battles of Chippewa and Niagara, July 5–25, 1814, by *Furst*. Size, 40
2111 MAJ.-GEN. EDWARD P. GAINES; for his gallant defence of Fort Erie, Aug. 15, 1814. Size, 40
2112 MAJ.-GEN. PETER B. PORTER; commemorative of the victories at Chippewa, Niagara, and Erie, by *Furst*. Size, 40
2113 MAJ.-GEN. JACOB BROWN; for the same victories. Size, 40   *Haines*
2114 BRIG.-GEN. JAMES MILLER; for the same. Size, 40
2115 BRIG.-GEN. RIPLEY; on the same victories. Size, 40
2116 MAJ. ALEXANDER MACOMB; for gallant conduct at the battle of Plattsburg, Sept. 11, 1814, by *Furst*. Size, 40
2117 Duplicate, (on thicker planchet).
2118 MAJ.-GEN. ANDREW JACKSON; for his brave and successful repulse of the English troops in their attack upon New Orleans, Jan. 8, 1815. Size, 40
2119 MAJ.-GEN. ZACHARY TAYLOR; from the State of Louisiana, called the "Pelican Medal," the design having been taken from (or at least first appearing on) a medal of Clement IX. Extremely fine, almost proof. Size, 48   *Farrier*
2120 LIEUT.-COL. BLISS; by the State of New York for services in Mexico. Size, 46   *Holland*
2121 MAJ.-GEN. GEORGE G. MEADE; by the United League of Philadelphia for services to the State of Penn'a at Gettysburg; obv. bust; rev. Liberty presenting Gen'l Meade a civic crown. Very beautiful medal, by *Pacquet*. Size, 52   *Nelson*
2122 Same, in tin.
2123 WINFIELD SCOTT; "From Virginia"; a beautiful medal by Wright. Splendid proof, scarce. Size, 56   *Armstrong. Lewis*
2124 GEN. ARMSTRONG; for the total destruction of Kittaning (by fire), Sept. 8, 1756. By the Corporation of the City of Philadelphia. Size, 30
2125 Medal of the Tayleur Fund for the succor of shipwrecked strangers. Scarce. Size, 28

NAVY.

2126 CAPT. JOHN PAUL JONES, of the "Bon Homme Richard," for the capture of the English frigate "Serapis," on the 23d of September, 1779. Size, 35

2127 CAPT. THOMAS TRUXTON; for good conduct in the action between the frigates "Constellation" and "La Vengeance," March 24, 1800. Size, 35
2128 Duplicate.
2129 Another, from broken die.

2130 CAPT. ISAAC HULL; for the capture of the "Guerriere," Jan. 29, 1813. Size, 40

2131 CAPT. JACOB JONES; for the capture of the "Frolic," Oct. 18, 1812. Size, 40

2132 CAPT. STEPHEN DECATUR; for the capture of the frigate "Macedonian," Oct. 25, 1812. Size, 40

2133 CAPT. WILLIAM BAINBRIDGE; for the capture of the British frigate "Java," Dec. 29, 1812. Size, 40
2134 Duplicate.

2135 CAPT. JAC. LAWRENCE; for the capture of the British brig "Peacock," Feb. 24, 1813. Size, 40

2136 LIEUT. W. BURROUGHS; for the capture of the sloop "Boxer," Jan. 6, 1814. Size, 40

2137 LIEUT. EDWARD R. McCALL; for the capture of the same sloop. Size, 40

2138 CAPT. OLIVER HAZARD PERRY; in honor of the victory on Lake Erie, Jan. 31, 1814, by the State of Pennsylvania. The reverse of the medal gives a picture of the battle. Size, 36

2139 Another, from same State; different reverse, in silver. Very rare.

2140 MULE, from the reverses of last two. Rare.

2141 PERRY; from Congress; rev. naval action. Size, 42

2142 CAPT. LEWIS WARRINGTON; for the capture of the brig-of-war "Epervier," Mar. 29, 1814. Size, 40

2143 CAPT. JOHNSON BLAKELY; for the capture of the sloop-of-war "Reindeer," Nov. 3, 1814. Size, 40

2144 CAPT. THOMAS MACDONOUGH; for the victory on Lake Champlain, Sept. 11, 1814. Size, 40

2145 CAPT. HENLY; EAGLE, for the same victory. Size, 40

2146 LIEUT. STEPHEN CASSIN; for the same. Size, 40

2147 CAPT. CHARLES STEWART; for the capture of the British ship-of-war "Cyane," Feb. 20, 1815. Size, 40

2148 COM. EDWARD PREBLE; for gallantry before Tripoli, 1804. Fine proof, very rare. Size, 40

2149 Same, gilt.

2150 Duplicate, in bronze. Fine proof.

Presidential and Political.

2151 BRIG SOMERS; medal for the rescue of her officers and men in the harbor of Vera Cruz, Dec. 10, 1846. C. C. Wright. Size, 36
2152 TESTIMONIAL to Captains Crichton, Low, and Stouffer, from the City of Philadelphia. Size, 48
2153 Duplicate.
2154 COMMODORE M. C. PERRY; from the merchants of Boston, for services in the treaty with Japan. Size, 40
2155 CAPT. INGRAHAM; for protecting Martin Kosta in the harbor of Smyrna. Size, 64
2156 Duplicate.
2157 ROBERT M. PATTERSON, Director of the U. S. Mint, 1835–51. Bronze. Size, 40
2158 Duplicate.
2159 GEN. ALEX. HAMILTON, SEC. TREAS UNIT STA; rev. edifice, 1795. Fine proof; bronze. Size, 32
2160 COMM'R DECATUR and Capt. Lawrence; busts opposite sides; tin. Very fine; rare. Size, 22

Presidential and Political.
[All unsoiled when not defined.]

WASHINGTON (1st Prest.)
2161 Bust; rev. residence at Mt. Vernon, G. II. S. Tin. Size, 22. 3 pieces
2162 Lovell's series of head quarters, in copper. Size, 18–10 pieces
2163 Bust; rev. bust of Lincoln; silver. Size, 12
2164 Bolen's Washington and others; a beautiful set of medals; copper. Size, 16. 6 pieces

JOHN ADAMS (2d Prest.)
2165 Bust; rev. residence; tin. Size, 22. 2 pieces

THOMAS JEFFERSON (3d Prest.)
2166 Bust; rev. residence; tin. Size, 22. 3 pieces
2167 Bust; rev. shield; silver. Size, 12. 2 pieces

JAMES MADISON (4th Prest.)
2168 Bust; rev. residences of Madison and Jackson; tin. Size, 22. 3 pieces

ANDREW JACKSON (7th Prest.)
2169 Bust of "Young Hickory"; rev. bust of ? by *R. L.* Tin, pierced and battered, but rare. Size, 24
2170 Bust; rev. residence; tin. Size, 22
2171 A number of contemporary medalets in brass and one in copper, no two alike. From fair to fine condition; two rare. 6 pieces

2172 Bust to l.; rev. eagle within circle of stars; pierced, not worn. Very rare and valuable; tin. Size, 25
2173 Bust; rev. inscription; silver. Size, 12.   3 pieces

Martin Van Buren (8th Prest.)

2174 Bust; rev. eagle, "The country demands," etc.; tin. Scarce.   Size, 23
2175 Bust; rev. residence; tin.   Size, 22
2176 Bust; rev. scales, "Our principles are justice and equality"; tin. Poor; rare.   Size, 24
2177 Bust; rev. safe, "Safe bind, safe find." Fair; tin. Rare.   Size, 23
2178 Bust, "The Fearless Democrat"; rev. ins.; copper, brass, and tin. Size, 23.   3 pieces
2179 A number of medalets in copper and brass.   4 pieces

Wm. Henry Harrison (9th Prest.)

2180 To commemorate the Young Men's Convention, 4th May, 1840; rev. large log-house, showing end and front, "To let, possession given in 1841"; raised and beveled rim, decorated on both sides with stars; pierced. Very fine and extremely rare.   Size, 28
2181 Duplicate, not as fine.
2182 Bust, nearly full face; rev. eight Presidents in medallions; an original proof impression from the dies, executed in 1840 by Bridgen, N. Y. Tin; *rare to excess.*   Size, 30

[The reverse of this medal has been restruck, but there are no new impressions of the piece as here described. It would be unsafe to call the medal unique, but the writer has not found a collector who knows of the existence of another.]

2183 Bust to left; rev. log cabin, flag flying to l. and file of nine soldiers; as fine as when struck. Very rare: tin.   Size, 24
2184 A similar medal, without the soldiers. Equally fine.
2185 Bust to right within circle of stars; rev. a small log-cabin just below the centre of the field, inscription in five straight and two curving lines:

Born
Feb. 9, 1775.
1811 TIPPECANOE
1813 FORT MEIGS
THAMES
(Log Cabin)
1840
PRESIDENTIAL CANDIDATE

Tin. Size, 24. Excessively rare and as fine as when struck.

2186 Bare bust to r. (unlike last); rev. same as last. Believed to be unique. *Hazeltine*
2187 Same obv. as 2185; rev. eagle within circle of stars. Tin. Size, 24
[The obverse of this medal was from the old die; the reverse was made to take the place of the original, which was never found.]
2188 Same in copper.
2189 Bust to left; rev. monument on Bunker Hill; struck to commemorate the jubilee Sept. 10, 1840. Original in tin, with loop and ribbon. Size, 28
2190 Same in silver, restruck. Brilliant proof. *Armstrong*
2191 Duplicate in tin (original).
2192 Same in lead, restruck.
2193 Bust to r. bare; rev. "candidate of the people," log cabin with bee-hive at one end and cider-barrel at the other; in white copper. Never before sold. Size, 16 *Proskey Parish*
2194 Same, in brass; pierced.
2195 Bust; reverse. "*Battle of the Thames, October* 5, 1813." By Congress. Uncirculated; copper. Size, 20
2196 Same, in German silver; pierced.
2197 BUNKER HILL; "A Nation's Gratitude." In copper, brass, and tin. Size, 24. 3 pieces
2198 Obverse of same. Reverse, Henry Clay. Copper.
2199 SABBATH-School Jubilee, in copper, nickel, brass, and tin. Size, 22. 4 pieces
2200 Obverse of the same medal; reverse blank. Copper, nickel, brass, and tin. 4 pieces
2201 Same obverse; reverse, log cabin. "THE PEOPLE'S CHOICE." Copper, brass, and tin. 3 pieces
2202 Reverse of last; muled with reverse of 2199; copper, nickel, brass, and tin. 4 pieces
2203 Same obverse; reverse, "He is a Freeman whom the Truth makes free." Copper, nickel, brass, and tin. 4 pieces
2204 Obverse, same as reverse of 2201; reverse same as last. Copper, nickel, brass, and tin. 4 pieces
2205 Obverse, "The People's Choice;" reverse blank. Copper, nickel, brass, and tin. 4 pieces
2206 Bust; reverse blank. Silver. (Ten struck.)
2207 Obverse; "The People's Choice;" log cabin; reverse blank. Silver. (Ten struck.) *Hollan*
2208 Bust within wreath of roses; reverse, residence. Tin, Size, 22
2209 HARRISON MEDALETS, in copper, brass, and tin. In beautiful uncirculated condition. 8 pieces
2210 Same, not so fine. Some rare. 10 pieces

HENRY CLAY.

2211 Set from Betts' dies, in copper, lead, and tin. Size, 28. 4 pieces

2212 Bust; reverse, angel standing by a monument, "EVERY END HE AIMED AT WAS HIS COUNTRY'S." Tin. Size, 28

2213 Small bust to left, within bunches of oak; reverse, inscription in parallel lines, circumscribed by, "Nominated by the Baltimore Convention, May 1st, 1844." Tin. *Extremely rare.* Size, 24

2214 Same, restruck in copper.

2215 Same obverse; reverse blank; restruck in tin and lead. 2 pieces

2216 Same obverse; reverse, Bunker Hill, "A NATION'S GRATITUDE." Copper.

2217 Obverse same as reverse of last; reverse same as reverse of No. 2213. Brass.

2218 Obverse, bust to right; reverse, Baltimore Monument. Bronze. Size, 24

2219 Same in Tin.

2220 Bust circumscribed, "Born and died," etc; reverse, "The Constitution, the Union, and Protection to Home Industry." Brass and tin. Size, 22. 2 pieces

2221 Same in silver. Extremely rare.

2222 Bust to left, by *True;* reverse, within a border of scrolls, flags, shields, etc., "EQUAL AND FULL PROTECTION," etc. Tin. Size, 22

2223 Bare bust to right, reverse, "LET US ENCOURAGE OUR OWN MANUFACTURES." Tin. Size, 22

2224 Bust; "A HALO SHINES AS BRIGHT AS DAY," etc; reverse, eagle on agricultural shield, "PROTECTION TO THE WORKING CLASSES." Tin. Size, 22

2225 Bust, "THE STAR OF THE WEST;" reverse, "United we stand, divided we fall." Tin. Size, 20

2226 Bust; reverse, "The Eloquent Defender of National Rights." Copper and Tin. Size, 20. 2 pieces

2227 Bust; reverse, "The Eloquent Advocate of Protection to Home Industry." In copper, brass, and tin. 3 pieces

2227*Duplicate set. Same in all respects. 3 pieces

2228 Same, in brass and copper. 2 pieces

2229 Same in silver. Extremely rare.

2230 Small bust, within two branches of oak, "PRESIDENT HENRY CLAY, 1843;" reverse, Eagle pierced. Tin. Extremely rare. Size, 14

2231 Same, not pierced.

2232 A similar piece, but not identical; different portrait. Tin, pierced, extremely rare.

Whig Medalets.

2233 BARE BUST; "In memory of Henry Clay"; reverse, "APRIL 12, 1860, New Orleans, La." Tin. Size, 15
[A remarkable and perhaps unique piece.]
2234 BUST; reverse, "A tariff for protection," and other pieces in different metals. In extremely fine condition. Size, 16. 6 pieces
2235 BUST; reverse, "The Mill-boy of the Slashes." Medalets, brass. 8 pieces
2236 CLAY Medalets from new dies, in different metals; struck on thick planchets, with various shells. Fine lot. 12 pieces

Whig Medalets.

2237 "FOR THE CONSTITUTION HURRA!" ship; rev. "Whigs of New York victorious, *Les trois jours*, April 8, 9, and 10, 1834." Brass, fine and rare. Size, 16
2238 "THE GLORIOUS WHIG VICTORY OF 1834"; illuminated Liberty cap; rev. "Fellow Citizens, save your Constitution"; ship. Copper, uncirculated, very rare. Size, 16
2239 Same, in tin. Brilliant, *excessively* rare.
2240 Duplicate of 2238. Very fine.
2241 GULIAN C. VERPLANK, our next Gov'r. Copper, pierced, rare. Size, 16

LEWIS CASS.

2242 BUST; rev. "The Sub-Treasury and the Tariff of Forty-six," by *Leonard*, on thick planchet. Tin. Size, 26
2243 Bust to r.; rev. "The Constitution and the Freedom of the Seas." In copper and tin. Size, 20. 2 pieces
2244 Medalets in brass. 2 pieces

WINFIELD SCOTT.

2245 Bust; rev. tablet on flags, etc, "Chippewa, Lundy's Lane, Vera-Cruz, and Mexico," by *Leonard*. Copper. Size, 26
2246 Same, in tin, *extra thick*.
2247 Others from same dies. Copper and tin. 2 pieces
2248 Bust; rev. "United we Stand," etc.; fasces on a star. In copper, brass, and tin. Size, 20. 3 pieces
2249 Same obverse; rev. ins. in six lines; with one, "Our Next President." Tin. 2 pieces
2250 Duplicate set; same as 2248. 3 pieces
2251 Another, with "Scott Wounded at Lundy's Lane." In brass and nickel, or white copper. 5 pieces

2252 Bust within branches of oak ; rev. "Nominated by the Baltimore Convention, 1852." Fine proof, copper. Size, 22
2253 Medalets in copper, brass, and tin. 4 pieces
2254 Scott Wounded at Lundy's Lane. In tin, on *thick* planchet, rare, and another. 2 pieces

DANIEL WEBSTER.

2255 Bust; rev. E. Hill's card. Tin. Size, 18. 2 pieces

JAMES K. POLK (11th President).

2256 Bust vis-a-vis with Geo. M. Dallas, by *Wagner*. Tin. Size, 28
2257 Duplicate.
2258 Shell; bust; rev. Young Hickory.

GEO. M. DALLAS.

2259 Bust; rev. "United We Stand," etc., and on a shield garnished with flags, "Our Country right or wrong." Tin. Size, 26
2260 Same obverse; rev. a space enclosed by branches of oak, uninscribed. Copper, with duplicate of last. 2 pieces

ZACHARY TAYLOR.

2261 Bust; rev. "Entered, according to Act of Congress, by Wm. G. Brown, in the Clerk's Office, District of Columbia." Tin. Size, 27
2262 Bust; rev. "I ask no favors," etc. Copper. Size, 26
2263 Same obverse; rev. uninscribed.
2264 Bust; rev. Fields fought in Mexico. Tin. Size, 24
2265 Bust; rev. "In honor of the Hero of Palo Alto," etc. Rare, tin. Size, 22
2266 Bust; rev. "A little more grape, Capt. Bragg." In copper and tin. Size, 20. 2 pieces
2267 Bust; rev. "Fort Harrison, O'Kee-cho-Bee," etc. In brass and tin. Size, 20. 2 pieces
2268 Medalets and shell. Fine and rare lot. 3 pieces

MILLARD FILLMORE (13th President).

2269 Bust; rev. residence. In copper and tin. Size, 22. 2 pieces
2270 Bust to r.; with'n wreath of oak leaves. "Be Vigilant and Watchful," etc., by *F. B. S. and H.* Copper. Size, 22
2271 Same; in tin.
2272 Bust, bare; rev. The Union; constellation; by *Odling*. Tin. Size, 24
2273 Same, but different reverse, with medalets. 3 pieces

JOHN C. FREMONT.

2274 Bust; "Honor to whom honor is due," castle on a mountain, engineers in foregrovnd, by *H. H.* Tin. Size, 28

2275 Bust; three-quarter face, THE COMING MAN; rev. " born;" " Jessie's Choice;" " planted the Stars and Stripes," etc., etc.; copper. Size, 26

2276 Same; in brass.
2277 Same; in tin.
2278 Set of last three; copper, brass, and tin. 3 pieces
2279 Bust; three-quarter face; FREE SPEECH, FREE PRESS, FREMONT; rev. Fremont and his party raising the Stars and Stripes on the Rocky Mountains, FREMONT and COCHRANE; copper. Size, 22

2280 Same; in brass.
2281 Same; in tin.
2282 Bust to r.; rev. "Free Soil," etc., by *F. B. S. & H.*; copper. Size, 22
2283 Same; in tin.
2284 Same, obverse; "Elect me President," etc.; in copper and tin. 2 pieces
2285 Medalets; in brass. 3 pieces

FRANKLIN PIERCE (14th President).

2286 Bust; three-quarter face; rev. eagle, " Pierce and King the people's choice "; copper, brass, and tin. Size, 18. 3 pieces

JAMES BUCHANAN (15th President).

2287 Bust to r.; rev. within wreath of oak, "The Crisis demands his Election"; copper. Size, 22
2288 Same; in tin, with medalet. 2 pieces

JOHN BELL.

2289 Bust; For President, John Bell of Tennessee; rev. eagle; tin. Size, 24
2290 Bust; rev. bust of Edward Everett; copper. Size, 20
2291 Same as last, with duplicate of 2289. 2 pieces
2292 Bust to l.; rev. "The Constitution, etc., Now and Forever"; in copper, brass, nickel, and tin. Size, 18. 4 pieces
2293 A number of mules from these and other dies, by *R. L.*, Philadelphia; one with reverse of Lincoln; scarce lot; copper and brass. 7 pieces
2294 Medalets in copper, nickel, and brass, some with reverse of Breckinridge, Lincoln, and Douglass. Rare lot. 12 pieces

JOHN C. BRECKINRIDGE.

2295 Bust; rev. eagle, by *True;* tin. Size, 24
2296 Bust; rev. "Our Country and Our Rights," on thick brass planchet, milled edge. Scarce. Size, 16
2297 Medalets similar in character to lot 2294. 12 pieces

STEPHEN A. DOUGLAS.

2298 Bust; full-face; rev. "Democratic Candidate for 16th President," by *Henning & Eyman;* tin. Size, 24
2299 Duplicate; pierced.
2300 Bust to l.; rev. eagle, by *True;* tin. Size, 24
2301 Bust to l.; rev. "Popular Sovereignty," etc., 1860; tin, by *Childs.* Size, 22
2302 Same obverse; rev. "Born April 23, 1813; Died June 3, 1861." Tin.
2303 Bust; full-face; rev. ins., "Support the Little Grant," etc.; in white copper and brass. Size 20. 2 pieces
2304 Same; rev. "The Champion of Popular Sovereignty"; in copper, nickel, brass, and tin. Size, 18. 4 pieces
2305 Medalets, by *Merriam, Jensch,* and others, in copper, brass, and tin. Av. size, 16. 5 pieces
2306 Smaller; similar to 2294; valuable lot. 16 pieces

ABRAHAM LINCOLN (16th President).

2307 Medal by the American Numismatic and Archæological Society, New York, 1866. Brilliant proof, silver; very rare. *(reduced size)* Size, 22
2308 Same; in copper.
2309 Same; in tin.
2310 Bust to r.; rev. two rails crossed, "Freedom and Protection," with ribbon; tin. Size, 24
2311 Bust; rev. laurel wreath and shield, inclosing ins., Republican Candidate, etc., by *Henning & Eyman;* pierced, tin. Size, 24
2312 Bust to l.; rev. "The Rail Splitter of 1830," a man splitting rails before sunrise on a prairie, by *Childs;* tin. Size, 26
2313 Bust to l.; rev. inscription within a rail fence, 1860; copper. Size, 22
2314 Same; in brass.
2315 Same; silver-plated and in tin. 2 pieces
2316 Same; in copper and tin. 2 pieces
2317 Bust; rev. 1861, "The right man in the right place"; copper. Size, 22
2318 Same; in brass.
2319 MERRIAM'S Medal; rev. his card, in copper and tin. Size, 20. 2 pieces

Key's Medal ; rev. head of Washington on a star,
"Freedom to all Men " ; tin.   Size, 20
Bust ; (*J. D. L.*) rev. " Let Liberty be National and
Slavery Sectional," " Our Next President," " United
we Stand, Divided we Fall," " No More Slave Terri-
tory "; tin. Size, 20.   4 pieces
Bust ; rev. busts of Washington and Lincoln, " The
Father—The Saviour of his Country"; tin bronzed
and tin. Size 22.   2 pieces
Bust ; " Honest Old Abe "; rev. Union Candidates, etc.,
with duplicate, by *J. D. L.* ; tin. Size, 22x20. 2 pieces
Bust ; " A Foe to Traitors "; rev. May the UNION
Flourish ; tin.   Size, 20
Bust ; rev. bust of Washington in starry robe, " The
Union Must and Shall be Preserved"; tin with rib-
bon.   Size, 18
Same as last, with Merriam's card ; in copper, brass, and
tin.   4 pieces
Bust to r. 1860 ; rev. " The man that can split rails or
guide the ship of State" ; in copper and brass. Size,
20.   2 pieces
Bust, 1860 ; rev. " Free Homes for Free Men"; in cop-
per, nickel, brass, and tin. Size, 18.   4 pieces
Bust to the waist ; " The rail splitter of the West," man
and boy splitting rails ; copper, brass, and white cop-
per. Size, 18.   3 pieces
Bust ; below, **25** ; IN GOD WE TRUST ; rev. eagle.
Size, 16 ; in tin ; rare.
Same ; in tin gilt, with a variety of others ; in copper,
brass, and lead.   6 pieces
Bust ; rev. " Freedom National," etc., on thick planch-
ets ; brass and tin. Size, 16.   2 pieces
Oval medalet, with loop ; struck in Geneva ; bust ; rev.
" Martyr to Liberty" ; copper. bronze   Size, 16x12
Duplicate of last, with reverse of flags and cannon ; in
copper, brass, and tin.   4 pieces
Same as last ; in copper, brass, and tin ; one with loop.
  4 pieces
Medalets, similar to 2294.   7 pieces
—— " Wide Awakes," etc.   8 pieces
Bust ; vis-a-vis with bust of Johnson ; rev. Rep. can-
didates, 1864 ; tin.   Size, 26
Silver medalet, struck at the mint after his assassina-
tion.   Size, 12
Set of similar medalets ; in silver, copper, and tin ; very
beautiful ; few struck. Size, 10.   3 pieces

ANDREW JOHNSON.

2341 BANQUET in New York, Aug. 29, 1866; bust; rev. shield and ins.; in silver, copper, and tin; few struck. Size, 20.   3 pieces

2342 Another set; silver, copper, and tin.   3 pieces

2343 Melanotypes, in the form of pins, or with loops, of Lincoln, Johnson, H. W. Beecher, and McClellan.   12 pieces

GEORGE B MCCLELLAN.

2344 MILITARY bust; rev. Bombardment of Fort Sumter, 1861; silver.   Size, 22

2345 Same; bust; rev. "one flag and one Union;" Eagle displayed; tin.   Size, 22

2346 Same; in copper.

2347 SIMILAR obverse; rev. "My Country I am sworn to defend"; tin. Size, 22.   2 pieces

2348 BUST to l.; rev. The people's choice for President, 1864; tin.   Size, 20

2349 BUST; rev. Washington in starry robe, and two others.   3 pieces

2350 BUST; rev. Knickerbocker; silver.   Size, 12

U. S. GRANT, (18th President.)

2351 BUST; full face, 1868; rev. "I propose to fight it out on this line if it takes all Summer"; silver. Size, 18; thick.

2352 Same; in copper.

2353 Same; in brass.

2354 Same; on extra thick planchet; tin.

2355 Bust to l.; rev. "Republican Candidate," etc.; silver.   Size, 18

2356 Same; in copper, brass, and tin.   3 pieces

2357 Bust to r.; within concentric circles of stars and laurels; rev. shield on flags; tin.   Size, 25

2358 Bust to l.; Rep. Candidate, etc.; rev. "I intend," etc.; in copper, brass, and tin.   3 pieces

2359 Same; in silver; rare.

2360 Bust to l.; Rev. U. S.; rev. surrender of Gen. Lee; rev. bust of Washington, with duplicate of 2358; in tin; two in brass, two in tin.   4 pieces

2361 MEDALETS; in silver, copper, brass, and tin; struck at the mint. Size, 12.   4 pieces

2362 Bust to r.; rev. Capture of Richmond; tin.   Size, 20

Army Officers.

- 2363 GRANT and COLFAX, with bust of Grant; rev. "The Hope of the Nation," "Match Em," etc.; tin. 3 pieces
- 2364 Same; with their busts accolated, 1868; rev. Let us have peace; silver; by *J. E. E.*; rare. Size, 18
- 2365 Similar obv. (with maker's imprint); rev. "General Amnesty," etc.; silver; same size; rare.
- 2366 Same as 2364; in copper, brass, and tin. 3 pieces
- 2367 Same as 2365; in copper, brass, and tin. 3 pieces
- 2368 SCHUYLER COLFAX; bust, full-face, 1868; rev. "Loyalty shall govern the Nation"; silver; same size as last; rare.
- 2369 Same; in copper, brass, and tin. 3 pieces
- 2370 SIGEL's medal of Grant and Colfax; rev. "For President and Vice-President, 1869–1873"; tin. Size, 24

SEYMOUR AND BLAIR.

- 2371 HORATIO SEYMOUR; rev. Democratic Candidate; silver; by *N. H. Key*; rare. Size, 18
- 2372 Same; in copper, brass, and tin. 3 pieces
- 2373 SIGEL's medal; same style as 2370; busts of Seymour and Blair accolated, or conjoined; rev. same as 2370; tin. Size, 24
- 2374 HORATIO SEYMOUR, by *Jacobus*; bust, full-face; rev. "White men to govern," etc.; tin. Size, 20
- 2375 Medalets (H. S.); in silver, copper, brass, and tin. Size, 12. 4 pieces

HORACE GREELEY.

- 2376 Bust; rev. same as 2371; tin. Size, 18
- 2377 Bust; rev. "Liberal Republican Candidate," etc.; tin. Size, 18
- 2378 Bust; rev. bust of B. Gratz Brown; tin. Size, 18

HENRY WILSON.

- 2379 Bust; rev. bust of Gen. Grant; tin. Size, 18

Army Officers.

- 2380 GEN. BURNSIDE: bust, full face; rev. record of battle fields, 1862; tin. Rare. Size, 24
- 2381 GEN. KEARNEY, by *Merriam*; rev. eagle, etc.; brass. Size, 20
- 2382 GEN. HOOKER, by same; rev. same; brass. Size, 20
- 2383 GEN. HUMPHREYS; rev. Trefoil? Tin. Size, 20
- 2384 GEN. GEARY; rev. star, "I vote as I fight." Size, 20
- 2385 GEN. BERRY; rev. "Killed at Chancellorville," etc. Copper. Size, 18
- 2386 Same, in bronze.

2387 GEN. PETER LYLE, (For Sheriff); rev. 28 battles. Brass, rare. Size, 18
2388 HEISTER CLYMER, (For Governor); rev. "All powerful when united." Tin. Size, 20

Patriotic Tokens.
[WITH A FEW NOT SO PATRIOTIC.]

2389 JEFFERSON DAVIS; rev. Death to Traitors, War for the Union, etc., etc. 5 pieces
2390 "I AM READY," "War of 1861," etc., etc. 5 "
2391 "HARTFORD Wide Awakes." In copper, brass, and white metal. 3 pieces
2392 "CONCESSION before Secession"; in silver, nickel, copper, brass, and tin. Size, 12. 5 pieces
2393 "UNION LEAGUE," Phila.; rev. Organized Dec. 27, '62, with loop; Loyal National do. Tin. 2 pieces
2394 WAR FUND Committee Medal; Honor to the Brave. Size, 26
2395 "OUR NEXT President"; rev. Boy and Dog; several varieties, in copper and tin; with "I am ready," and "The wealth of the South." 7 pieces
2396 "THE FIRST battle between Iron-clad war vessels"; rev. ins., silver. Scarce. Size, 20
2397 JOHN BROWN; rev. his gallows. Tin. Size, 20
2398 GEN. WAYNE, Clay, Tom Thumb, and others. 6 pieces
2399 KOSSUTH; (one variety, said to be *rare*); California counters, etc. 6 pieces

Miscellaneous.

2400 WASHINGTON Calendars, two varieties; brass. Size, 22. 2 pieces
2401 PARTHENON, New York, 1825; rev. "Admit the bearer," etc.; two varieties of Peale's Museum check. Rare and very fine, copper. Size, 22. 2 pieces
2402 "FIRST Steam Coinage," March 23, 1836. Copper, proof.
2403 WOOD'S Minstrels Check; silver, uncirculated. 2 pieces
2404 FEUCHTWANGER's composition, 2 Courtland St., New York. Very rare, fine. Size, 18
2405 Same; with his address, 377 Broadway. Equally rare and still finer.
2406 W. B. CHAPMAN, 6th and Vine Sts., Phila., "One glass of Soda or Blue Lick Water"; other cards proffering

Miscellaneous. 113

similar beverages, from branches of the same establishment, as for example, T. B. Harris, A. M. Stevens, W. J. M. Gordon; in same composition as last. 4 rare cards.

2407 "The Gift of Franklin"; pens crossed above an open book; rev. "Adjudged by the School Committee," etc.; *James Vila*, 1802. Very rare, silver. Size, 22

2408 Lynchburg Agricultural and Mech. Soc.; silver medal, uninscribed. Rare. Size, 24

2409 New Jersey State Agricultural Soc.; Silver, uninscribed, rare. Same size.

2410 New York State Agricultural Soc., uninscribed; with Reward of Merit Medals, in tin. 5 pieces

2411 Fulton Institute, Lancaster, Pa.; bust of Fulton; rev. Awarded to ———. Fine proof, tin. Size, 32

2412 Mass. Hort. Soc.; bust of Sam'l Appleton, 1845; rev. uninscribed. Rare, bronze. Size, 26

2413 Middlesex Mech. Ass., Lowell, Mass.; arm wielding hammer. Uninscribed, bronze. Size, 26

2414 Worcester High School; Bullock medal, 1859. Bronze, uninscribed. Size, 26

2415 Warren & Son, Sacramento City, Cal.; uninscribed, tin. Size, 26

2416 Maine Charitable Mech. Ass.; uninscribed, copper. Size, 20

2417 Cincinnati, 1870, '71, and '72, Industrial Exposition. Tin. 4 pieces

2418 H. Miller & Co., Louisville, Ky.; to commemorate the Mechanics' Fair, 1858; in copper, brass, and tin. A medal of very excellent work. Size, 22. 3 pieces

2419 Boston City Medal, "For the males"; Lozenge stamp, with R. Hill's card, etc. 4 pieces

2420 Bunker Hill Fair, Sep. 8, 1840; Death of Warren and view of the monument, by *Mitchell;* copper. Very fine and rare. Size, 28

2421 Same, in tin; pierced.

2422 New Haven Numismatic Society, founded 1862. Tin. Size, 29

2423 Mobile Jockey Club, members' medal; rev. not transferable, 1853. Silver, rare. Size, 17

2424 Same, in tin, with different reverses. 2 pieces

2425 R. Lovett's card; rev, Washington before Boston; silver, copper, brass, and tin. Rare. Size, 20. 4 pieces

2426 Fireman's Medal, 1860; "When duty calls we go." Silver. Size, 20

8

2427 Pioneer Base Ball Club, with Sage's card, and Great Eastern. Copper, brass, and tin. Size, 20. 4 pieces

2428 Atlantic Telegraph; "How are you, Jonathan." Copper and tin. Size, 20. 2 pieces

2429 Same, muled with boy and dog; in copper and tin. 4 pieces

2450 Great air-ship City of New York, etc. 5 pieces

2451 Slave Trade abolished by Great Britan, 1807; "We are all brethern"; scene on a plantation, proprietor and slave shaking hands. Beautiful proof, bronze. Size, 23

2452 Edwin Forrest, Edward Everett, and Stephen Girard. Bronze. Size, 20. 3 pieces

2453 John Allan; rev. John K. Curtis' card. Brass and tin. Size, 20. 2 pieces

2454 "We all have our hobbies"; dedicated to coin collectors; (the device of a devil riding a broom). Copper, nickel, brass, and tin. Size, 18. 4 pieces

2455 U. S. Armory, Springfield; reverse, view of the Arsenal. Copper and brass. Size, 18. 2 pieces

2456 Sage's numismatic gallery, with heads of Jeremiah Colburn, Winslow Lewis, Charles J. Bushnell, Frank Jandon, Robert J. Dodge, Henry Bogert, and William H. Chesley. Copper proofs. Size, 20. 7 pieces

2457 Sage's historical tokens; no duplicates; all fine proofs. Copper. Size, 20. 26 pieces

2458 J. W. Sheerer & Co., drayage checks for 10, 15, 20, and 25 cents; rare. Brass. Size, 20. 4 pieces

2459 A lot of Strasburgher and Nuhn spiel marks, etc., different sizes. Brass and copper. 12 pieces

2460 "Non Vi Virtute Vici," by Merriam, splendid proof, bronze. Size, 18

Silver Medalets and Tokens.

(Many of them rare and all fine proofs.)

2461 Major-General H. G. Berry; bust; reverse, killed at Chancellorville, Va., May, 1863. Size, 18

2462 M. L. Marshall's card, Oswego, N. Y., 1860. Size, 18

2463 U. S. Armory, Springfield; view of the arsenal. Size, 20

2464 H. Mulligan's card, Philadelphia. Size, 20

2465 Fireman's Medal, 1860. Size, 20

2466 American Institute Medal. Size, 20

2467 New Jersey State Agricultural Society. Size, 22

2468 The old Jersey Prison-ship; rev. Fanueil Hall, Boston, by G. H. L. Size, 20

2469 J. D. Lovett's card, 1 Courtlandt street. Size, 16
2470 Brimelow's card; three varieties. Rare. Size, 16
2471 "We all have our hobbies." Size, 17
2472 Wood's Minstrels admission ticket.
2473 Edward Cogan's card, 1860; fine proof on thick planchet. Size, 13
2474 Copy of the Lord Baltimore penny. Size, 13
2475 H. B. Melville, bust; rev., good for one cent. Size, 12
    2 pieces
2476 R. Lovett's card; fine head of Liberty, 1860. Size, 12
2477 Stephen A. Douglass; rev., Intervention is di-union. Size, 12
2478 Broas Bros., New York, one dime; rev., Benjamin Franklin; same, head of Franklin; rev. Penny saved is penny earned. Size, 12. 2 pieces
2479 Ed. Schaf, 14 & 16 Division st., N. Y., 1863. Size, 12
2480 J. H. Warner, 104 Barclay st. Size, 12
2481 The Federal Union, it must be preserved; equestrian figure; varieties. Size, 12. 4 pieces
2482 Head of Washington, encircled by laurels; rev. Monk's metal signs, and others. Size, 12. 4 pieces
2483 A similar lot; five varieties and pieces. Size, 12
2484 T. Ivory's card, Brooklyn, various reverses and styles; two in silver, one in nickel, two in brass. Size, 12
    5 pieces
2485 Monitor token; Union forever, 1863, with varieties of similar character; no duplicates. Size 12. 3 pieces
2486 Similar lot, our Navy, etc. Size, 12. 4 pieces
2487 Head with legend, Liberty and no slavery; other styles of Liberty head; rev. various reverses. 4 pieces
2488 Jackson medalet, struck at the mint, with T. Ivory's Washington token. Size, 12. 2 pieces
2489 R. Lovett, Jr.'s card. rev. St. George and the Dragon, with A knight; Prescott; and Keach's mineral water tokens. All rare. 4 pieces
2490 Robert Soulsby, Vauxhall; Suire Eckstein & Co., with a rare Louisville, Ky., token. 3 pieces

---

A Cabinet of Greek Medals of the Decadrachm and Tetradrachm size, reproduced in fac-simile by the electrotype process from unique and rare originals, in the British and other museums.

[It is only necessary to see a single tray of these beautiful coins to comprehend the superiority of Greek Art. Every other system seems, by comparison, either rude or overdone. The wonderful effects produced by a few unerring lines remain to the present day entirely unequalled. As a full and accurate description accompanies each piece, and will be delivered with it to the purchaser, it would seem quite unnecessary to do more than arrange the several lots in trays, each one free from duplicates, and leave to the buyer the selection of trays.]

2491 Decadrachm in silver of Athens, Syracuse, and Agrigentum; Tetradrachm of Antigonus, Amphipolus, Clazomene, Mansolus, Rhodes, Catana, Rheginm, Samos, Gnossus, Thurium, Thasus, Magnesia, Miletus, Perseus, Nicomedes, Prusias, Pharnaces, Attalus, Tigranes, etc., etc; superb gold medallion of Ptolemy III. with four heads. 40 pieces

2492 Similar lot; a continuation, containing the Syracuse medallion, with the hair in a *net*; the decadrachm of Panormus, Agregintum, etc., etc. 40 pieces

2493 Similar, with a number of remarkable Jewish coins in silver of the full shekel and half-shekel size; gold Stater of Alexander Magnus, etc., etc. 40 pieces

2494 Similar, containing a medallion (decadrachm) of Arsinoe, wife of Ptolemy II., with others of the same volume of Bisaltæ, Sicily, Persia, etc. 40 pieces

2495 Similar, containing a large number of the tetradrachms of Syria. 40 pieces

2496 Similar. 40 pieces

2497 Similar; no decadrachms. 60 pieces

2498 Final lot, gold and silver.

Collection of Store Cards, Tokens, Small Medals, and Copperheads, in different Metals, Copper, Nickel, Brass, and Tin.

[These various collections are arranged on perforated boards, in alphabetical or other appropriate order, according to class, size, or other qualities. The rarer pieces will in almost all cases be found present, and the condition uncirculated and bright.]

2499 Twenty-one boards, containing 804 pieces of the large copper cent size.

2500 Six boards, with 215 shin-plasters and rare tokens.

2501 Twenty-one boards, containing 1547 pieces; large and small copperheads.

CARDS AND COPPERHEADS IN SILVER.

2502 Alfred S. Robinson; rev. Granby cent.

2503 Basley & Co., Philadel'a; rev. watches, diamonds, pearls, etc. Size, 21

2504 T. Brimlow, druggist; rev. one glass soda.

2505 Wood's Minstrels token, 25 cents.

2506 T. Ivory; various copperheads. Rare. 3 pieces

2507 A selection; Brimlow's, Ivorie's and others. 7 pieces

Numismatic History and Text Books.

2508 Manual of Coins and Bullion, by ECKFELD and DUBOIS, with supplement to 1851. Philadelphia, 1851. Small folio, half morocco; illustrated.

American Coinage, by HICKCOX. Albany, 1858. Illustrated. Quarto, half morocco.
History of Paper Money issued by the State of New York from 1709-89, by HICKCOX. Albany, 1866. Quarto, paper.
Monograph of the Dollar, by J. L. RIDDELL. New Orleans, 1845. Illustrated. Oct., cloth. Rare.
Hand-Book of English Coins, by LLEWELLYNN JEWETT. London. Illustrated 12mo, cloth.
Coinage of Great Britain, by RUDING. London, 1819. Oct., half calf. 5 vols
Vol. of Plates to accompany Ruding's Coinage, etc. Small folio, bound in same style as 2513.
Essay on Medals, by JOHN PINKERTON. London, 1789. Illustrated. Oct., old calf. 2 vols.
Ackerman's Ancient Coins. London, 1846. Illustrated. Royal oct., cloth.
Ackerman's Coins of the Romans, relating to Britain. London, 1844. Illustrated. Oct., cloth.
Ackerman's Roman Coins. London, 1834. Illustrated. Royal oct., half morocco, 2 vols.
An Arrangement of Tradesmen's Cards, etc., by Chasf J. Bushnell. New York, 1858. Illustrated. 8vo, hal. morocco.
Medals of Washington, by James Ross Snowden. Phila., 1851. Illustrated. Quarto, cloth.
Description of antique medals, Greek and Roman, by Mionnet. Paris, 1806. Oct., boards half cloth, with additional vol. of plates, etc., 7 vols.
Same, with rarity and price, etc. Illustrated. Two vols. uniform with lot 2521.
Supplement to Mionnet's work. Paris, 1819. Illustrated. Oct., cloth, 9 vols.
Weight of Greek medals, silver and gold, by same. 1 vol., 8vo.
Atlas (Numismatic), by same. Paris, 1838. Folio.
Rarity and price of Roman medals. Paris, 1815, by same. Thick 8vo, half morocco.

[This magnificent work, comprising in all 21 vols., cost to import, without duty, £150, Gold.]

Traité Elémentaire De Numismatique Ancienne, etc., by Jacob J. Gerard. Paris, 1825. Illustrated. 8vo, two vols in one vol., half morocco. Rare.
Medaglie Del Musee Farnese, by Paoli Pedrusi. Parma, 1694. Illustrated. Folio, full morocco, gilt. Superb and rare work, 7 vols.

2529 La Sicilia Di Philippe Paruta. Lione, 1697. Folio. Illustrated. Full morocco. Rare.

2530 Recherches Sur Les Monnaies Lee la Presqu'ile Italique, Par L. Sanbon. Naples, 1670. Illustrated. Folio, paper.

2531 Table of the rarity and price of Roman Coins, by St. Dennis, (French.) Blois, 1849. Thin quarto, half morocco.

CATALOGUES.

1851.
2532 Doctor Lewis Roper, Phila. Rare.

1853 to '55.
2533 State Library; Dan'l E. Groux, etc., comprising many loose sheets, hand-bills, etc. The lot.

1858 and '9.
2534 H. H. Leeds, Chas. H. Morse (Cambridgeport), Wm. L. Bramhall, J. D. Foskett, etc. A rare lot.   16 pieces

1860.
2535 H. H. Leeds & Co. (oblong cat.), H. G. Dwenger, Wm. H. Dayton, etc., etc.   29 pieces

1861.
2536 Priced and unpriced (3 and 9).   12 pieces

1862.
2537 Priced, unpriced, and duplicates.   27 pieces

1863.
2538 Priced, unpriced, and duplicates.   37 pieces

1864.
2539 Priced, unpriced, and duplicates, comprising several very rare eg. broadside of Thomas & Sons, Philadelphia.   27 pieces

1865.
2540 Priced, unpriced, and duplicates (several broadsides).   23 pieces

1866.
2541 W. E. W. and R. B. Chambers and others.   10 pieces

1867.
2542 Dan Scott & Co., Chicago (rare), and others; several priced.   12 pieces

1868.
2543 Nippes and others.   4 pieces

1869.

M. L. Mackenzie, illustrated; E. J. Farmer (Cleveland),
J. W. Haseltine, Philadelphia, etc., etc.   Good lot.
                                               21 pieces
1870.

Comprising several that are scarce.   10 pieces
           1871 and '72.
Priced and unpriced.   13 pieces
               1873.
Illustrated, priced, etc.   24 pieces
           1874 and '5.
Illustrated, etc.   35 pieces

LARGE PAPER CATALOGUES.

Ed. Cogan. Oct. 18, 19, 1860. Priced.
Same. May 21, 22, '60. Not priced.
Finotti sale. Nov., 1862. Priced and interleaved. Rare.
W. E. Woodward. April, 1863. Priced and interleaved. Rare.
Thos. Birch & Son. April, 1870.
Few Smith cabinet. 1870.

Handsome solid mahogany cabinet with 80 drawers, arranged in two tiers; double doors and patent lock; *Strobridge*
standing five feet high; an exceptionally well made
and perfect article.   *(& Leap?)*
Smaller rosewood cabinet, with single door, covering 16
bird's-eye maple drawers, each containing five silk-lined   "
trays. Very convenient and pretty.
White wood cabinet; spaced for 62 slides, with two
deep drawers below; movable front.

(End of Friday's Sale)

ADDENDA.

Greek Coins.
Gold.

1. ALEXANDER (Magnus); obv. head of Pallas; rev. Victory, with crown, AΔEXANΔPOΨ Stater; struck at Sidon. Fine.

Silver.

2. MAGNESIA (Ionia); head of Diana; rev. Apollo nude beside trophy, MAGNHTΩN EPAΣIΠΠOE APIΣTEOY Very fine and rare. Tet.
3. PTOLEMY I. (Soter), B.C. 324; diademed head; rev. ΠTOΛEMAIOΓ ΣΩTHPOΣ, eagle standing on thunderbolt, in field; letters and monogram. Very fine and rare. Tet.
4. PTOLEMY I.; obv. same as 3; rev. ΠTOΛEMAIOY BAΣIΛEΩE, eagle on thunderbolt; in field, letter and monogram. Very fine, rare. Tet.
5. —— Like 4; differing only in letters and monograms. Fine. Tet.
6. —— Same.
7. —— Same.
8. —— Same.
9. —— Same.
10. —— Same, rusted, poor.
11. —— Obv. like 4; rev. ΠTOΛEMAIOΓ EΩTHPOE, eagle on thunderbolt. Fine, rare. Tet.
12. —— Differs from 11 only in letters in field, but not so fine.
13. PTOLEMY II., Auletes, B.C. 59; obv. laureated head; rev. eagle; struck in Phœnicia. Good, very rare. Tet.
14. ANTIOCHUS VII., Euergetes, B.C. 139; obv. head; rev. Pallas standing with victory and spear, BAΣIΛEΩE ANTIOXOΓ EYEPΓETOΓ in laurel crown. Tet. Very fine and very rare.
15. ANTIOCHUS VIII., Epiphanes, B.C. 124; obv. dia. head of King; rev. Jupiter sitting with Victory and spear, above his head thunderbolt, BAEIΛEΩΣ ANTIOXOΓ EΠI ΦANOΓΣ. Tet. Very fine and very rare.
16. Similar to 15. Poor.
17. DEMETRIUS I., Soter, of Syria, B.C. 162; obv. dia. head of King; rev. female sitting with rod and cornucopia; in field, monogram, BAΣIΛEΩΣ ΔHMHTPIOΓ ΣΩTHPOΣ. Very fine and very rare. Tet.

Addenda. 121

18 DEMETRIUS II., Nicator, of Syria, B.C. 146; obv. head of King; rev. eagle, ΔHMHTPIOΓ ΒΑΣΙΛΣΩΣ; in field, letters and monograms; struck at Tyre. Poor, very rare. Tet.

19 PHILIP, Epiphanes, of Syria, B.C. 93; obv. dia. head; rev. Jupiter sitting with Victory and spear; ΒΑΣΙΛΕΩΣ ΦΙΛΙΠΠΟΓ ΕΠΙ ΦΑΝΟΥΕ; in field, monogram. Poor, rare. Tet.

20 ALEXANDER MAGNUS, B.C. 336; Drachma. Poor.

21 ANTIGONAS GONATAS, Macedonia, B.C. 279; obv. head of Pan with horns, in centre of Macedonian shield; rev. Pallas hurling thunderbolt, and holding shield in left hand; ΒΑΣΙΛΕΩΣ ΑΝΤΙΓΟΝΟΓ; in field, helmet and letters. Very fine and very rare. Tet.

22 ARIOBARZANES I. of Cappadocia, B.C. 93; obv. head of King; rev. Pallas standing. Poor, rare. Tet.

23 ARSACES XV., Phraates, B.C. 37; obv. dia. head of King with beard; rev. King sitting, crowned by female holding cornucopia; ΒΑΣΙΛΕΩΣ ΑΡCΑΚΟΓΕΓ ΕΡΓΕΤΟΓ ΕΠΙΦΑΝΟΓΕ ΔΙΚΑΙΟΥ. Very fine and very rare. Tet.

24 ARSACES VI., B.C. 164; obv. head of King, with beard; rev. King sitting holding bow; ΒΑΣΙΛΕΩΣ ΒΑΣΙΛΕΩΝ ΜΕΓΑΛΟΥ ΑΡΣΑΚΟΥ ΕΠΙΦΑΝΟΥΣ; piece broken off, otherwise good. Drachm.

25 CHOSROES I., A.D. 530; obv. head of King, and Sassanian legend; rev. fire-altar between two Magi, Sassanian legend. Good and very rare. Tet.

26 HORMUZD IV., A.D. 579; obv. head of King, with diadem highly ornamented, and Sassanian legend within double circle ornamented with stars; rev. fire-altar between two Magi, within triple circle ornamented with stars. Tet. Fine and very rare.

27 ARTAXERXES, A.D. 226; obv. galley, with waves below; rev. two men standing facing each other; hemidrachma. Very fine and very rare.

28 ÆGINA; obv. tortoise; rev. punch marks. Rusted, but good, and rare obolus.

29 ATHENS; obv. head of Pallas; rev. owl in hollow square; archaic, drachma. Poor.

30 ATHENS; obv. head of Pallas; rev. owl on Diota; ΛΘΕ ΑΜΜΟΔΙΟ in laurel crown. Good. Tet.

31 DYRRUCHIUM ILLYRICUM; obv. cow suckling calf; rev. punch mark; drachma. Good and very rare.

32 ARADUS, Phœnicia; obv. bee; rev. stag standing, and palm-tree; ΑΡΑΔΙΩΝ, drachma. Good, rare.

33 NEAPOLIS, Campania; obv. head of Diana; rev. Minotaur crowned by Victory; didrachma. Good.
34 ACHÆAN League (Elis.); obv. head of Jupiter; rev. ins. in laurel crown; drachma. Poor, but rare.
35 TYRE; obv. laureated head of Hercules, or Baal; rev. eagle; TYPOY IEPAΣ KAI AΣYΛOY; in field, club, palm branch, and letters. Æra of Tyre (B.C. 106). Good and rare. Tet.
36 TYRE; similar to 35, except letters in field. False.
2 pieces

Roman and Greek Imperial.

SILVER.

37 CŒCILIA Family; head; rev. elephant MET, Denarius; pierced. Rare.
38 Sept Severus; rev. Apollo standing; denarius.
39 IMP'L of Alexandria; Tetradrachm of Augustus and Tiberius; obv. radiated head of Aug; rev. laureated head of Tib. Good, rare.
40 Same of Vespasian and Titus; obv. head of Vesp.; rev. head of Titus. Good, very rare. Tet.
41 Same of Nero and Poppœa; obv. head of Nero; rev. head of Poppœa; potin. Good and rare. Tet.
42 NERO; head; rev. veiled head of Juno of Argos. HPA APΓEIA, Potin. Fine and rare. Tet.
43 Imp'l of Nero; obv. head of Nero; rev. EIΠINII, Peace holding caduceus, etc., LΔ (year 4); potin.; good. Tet.
44 —— of Vespasian; obv. head of Vespasian; rev. eagle; silver; good. Tet.
45 —— of Otho; obv. laureated head of Otho; AΓOTOKP. ATΨP MAPKOE OΘΨN KAICAP CEBACTOC; rev. eagle standing on wreath; in field, palm branch, ΞTOYC A, (year 1); fine and very rare; silver. Tet.
46 —— of Trajan; obv. head of Trajan; rev. eagle standing on thunderbolt; in field, palm branch, and letters II P; good and rare. Tet.
47 Imp. Greek of Antioch, (Syria,) Trajan; obv. head of Trajan; rev. Pallas sitting, holding Victory; ΔEMAPX EΞ YΠAT Γ; fine, rare; silver. Tet.
48 —— of Trajan; obv. head of Trajan; rev. Distyle Temple; good, but rusted; very rare; silver. Tet.
49 —— of Sept. Severus; obv. head; rev. eagle; potin., rusted; rare.
50 —— of Caracalla; obv. head; rev. eagle; potin., fine.
51 —— of Caracalla; nearly same as 50, but not so fine.

Addenda. 123

52 Imp'l of Caracalla ; rev. eagle ; potin., good.
53 —— of Trajan Decius ; obv. head ; rev. eagle ; potin., fine
54 —— of Trajan Decius ; near same as 53, but not so fine.
55 —— of Trebonianus Gallus ; obv. head ; rev. eagle ; potin., fine.
56 Imp. Greek of Samosata Syria, of Philip, the Arabian ; obv. head of Philip ; rev. turretted female, sitting on a rock ; ΦΛ CAMOCAT EΨN ; good. Tet.
57 Seleucis, Syria; obv. veiled and turretted head of City ; rev. thunderbolt on table, ΣΕΛΕΥΚΕΩΝ ΤΗΣ ΙΕΡΑΣ ΚΑΙ ΑΥΤΟΝΟΜΟΥ ; Tet., fine and rare ; silver.

GREEK COPPER.

58 Corcyra ; obv. Diota, with star on each side ; rev. Diota, star on each side, 3d brass, fine and very rare.
59 Parthian ; obv. head of King ; rev. legend ; figure sitting ; 3d brass, poor.
60 Parthian ; obv. head of King ; rev. head of horse ; legend ; 3d brass, poor, very rare.
61 Seleucus, 2d, B.C. 247 ; obv. head of Diana ; rev. Apollo standing, leaning on tripod; ΒΑΣΙΛΕΩΣ ΣΕΛΕΥΚΟΥ. 2d brass, serrated, poor.
62 Demetrius I. of Syria ; obv. head of Diana ; rev. Tripod ; 1st brass, serrated ; poor, but rare.
63 Sassanian ; obv. head in circle, and Sassanian legend ; rev. type unknown ; Sassanian legend ; size, 1st brass ; poor.
64 Ephesus ; obv. Bee, EΦ ; rev. stag rising from ground ; 3d brass ; pierced ; rare.
65 Ptolemy ; obv. head of Jupiter Ammon ; rev. eagle ; very large size ; good.
66 —— Same ; fine.
67 —— Same ; good.
68 —— Same ; good.
69 —— Same ; good.
70 —— Same ; good.
71 —— Same ; first brass size ; fine.
72 —— Same ; first brass size ; fair.
73 —— Same ; first brass size ; poor.
74 Ptolemy 8th and 9th; same ; rev. 2 eagles; fair.
75 —— Same; rev. 2 eagles ; fair.
76 Antiochus IV. of Commagene ; obv. diademed head of King ; ΒΑΣΙΛΕΥΣ ΜΕΓΑΣ ΑΝΤΙΟΧΟΣ ; rev. ΚΟΜΜΑΓΗΝΩΝ ; scorpion, in laurel crown ; fine and rare.
77 Sidon ; obv. Temple of 4 columns ; rev. Europa on bull ; ΣΙΔΩΝΙΩΝ ; size, 2d brass ; fine and very rare.

78 SIDON; obv. turretted head of City; rev. Europa on bull; Phœnician legend; size, 3d brass; fine and very rare.
79 ADRAMYTIUM; obv. head of Palas; rev. owl on thunderbolt; size, 3d brass; good and very rare.
80 GAZA (Judea); obv. head of Hadrian; rev. figure standing; ΓΑΖΑ ΔΕΠΙΓ; imp. Greek; size, 3d brass; good and very rare.
81 ATTANIBILUS, King of Characene; obv. head of King; rev. man sitting on cortina; size, 2d brass; poor, very rare.
82 TRIPOLIS; obv. turretted head of City; rev. The Dioscuri on horseback; size, 3d brass; good, very rare.
83 COMMAGENE; obv. animal; rev. scorpion. Size, 3d b.; good, v. r.
84 TARSUS (Cilicia); obv. turretted female sitting; rev. Jupiter sitting with Victory; size, 2d b., poor, v. r.
85 PRUSIAS II., King of Bithynia; obv. head of King; rev. Jupiter standing with spear and crown; 2d b., fair.
86 EPHESUS; obv. head of Diana; rev. forepart of stag, ΕΦ size, 2d b.; good, rare.
87 ANTIOCHUS XI.; obv. head of King; rev. Victory standing; size, 3d b.; good, rare.
88 PTOLEMY, Antiochus VII; Tarsus, Seleucia, Philip V.; size, 2d and 3d b.; fair.   5 pieces
89 —— IX. Demetrius II. of Syria; Alexander Magnus, Seleucus II., Philip V.; size, 2d and 3d b.; fair.   5 pieces
90 —— Antioch, Alexander Magnus, Sidon, Marathus; size, 2d and 3d b.; fair, some rare.   5 pieces
91 —— IX.; Cassander, Antioch, Smyrna, Antiochus I.; size, 2d and 3d b.; good.   5 pieces
92 —— Tripolis, Apamea, Tryphon, Smyrna; 2d and 3d b.; good, some rare.   5 pieces
93 —— IX.; Alexander Bala, Seleucis in Pieria, Antiochus VII., Marathus; size, 2d and 3d b.; good, some rare.   5 pieces
94 —— Seleucis in Pieria, Antioch, Thyatira, Philip Aridaeus; size, 2d and 3d b.; fair.   5 pieces
95 ANTIOCH, Smyrna, Seleucis Pieria, Smyrna Alexander Magnus; size, 2d and 3d b.; poor.   5 pieces
96 PTOLEMY, Antioch, Selge, Antiochus VI., Alexander Bala: 2d and 3d b.; fair.   5 pieces
97 EPHESUS, Side, Amphipolis, Alexander Magnus, Philip V.; 3d b.; fair,   5 pieces
98 ANTIOCHUS I.; Epidaurus, Antiochus III., Cyme, Laodicea; 3d b.; fair.   5 pieces

Addenda. 125

99 HALICARNASSUS, Antiochus I., Ptolemy, Amisus, Berytus;
   3d b.; poor, some very rare. 5 pieces
100 GARGARA, Mytilene, Chios, Assus, Rhodes; 3d b.: good,
   some v. r. 5 pieces
101 TARSUS, Aradus, Ptolemy, Antiochus VII.; Alpamea;
   2d and 3d b.; •fair. 5 pieces
102 PTOLEMY, Philip V., Tripolis, Marathus, Aradus; 2d and
   3d b.; good, some very rare. 5 pieces
103 ARADUS, Antiochus VI., Alexander Magnus, Amisus,
   Sidon; 3d b.; fair. 5 pieces
104 SELEUCIS IN PIERIA, Ptolemy, Antioch, Elis, Assus; 2d
   and 3d b.; fair, some rare. 5 pieces
105 SELEUCIS PIERIA, Ptolemy, Phoenicia, Antioch, Zacyn-
   thus; 2d and 3d b.; some very rare. 5 pieces
106 ARADUS, Alexander Magnus, Ptolemy, Mytilene, Judea;
   2d and 3d b.: some good and very rare. 5 pieces
107 —— A lot of 2d and 3d size; most poor, some rare.
   10 pieces
108 —— A lot of 2d and 3d size; most poor, some very rare.
   10 pieces
109 —— A lot of 2d and 3d size; most of them of the
   Ptolemies; poor. 10 pieces
110 ROGER, Prince of Antioch; size, 2d b.; poor, rare.
111 ANTIOCHUS VIII., of Syria; and Philistis, wife of Hiero
   II.; fine, false. 3 pieces
112 —— A lot of 2d and 3d sizes; most of them coins of the
   Ptolemies; poor. 10 pieces
113 —— A lot of 2d and 3d sizes; most of them of the
   Ptolemies; poor. 11 pieces
114 JOTAPA (?); obv. female head; rev. head.

Alexandrian—Copper.

115 GALLIENUS, Salonina, Aurelian, Severina. Claudius
   Gothicus; fine, and some rare. 5 pieces
116 —— Salonina, Claudius Gothicus, Severina, Tacitus;
   some fine and rare. 5 pieces
117 Same; some fine. 5 pieces
118 Varieties; good. 5 pieces
119 ——   " 5 pieces
120 ——   " 5 pieces
121 ——   " 5 pieces
122 ——   " 5 pieces
123 ——   " 5 pieces
124 ——   " 5 pieces
125 ——   " 5 pieces
126 ——   " 5 pieces
127 ——   " 5 pieces
128 —— poor 6 pieces

Imperial Greek—Copper.

129 TRAJAN; obv. fair; rev. very fine, man standing on galley, holding crown; struck at Sidon, B.C. 85; patinated; very rare; size, 2d brass.
130 ANTIOCH, Trajan Decius; rev. figure wearing modius, in temple of 4 columns; below, figure representing river swimming; above temple a ram running; good, rare; size, 1st brass.
131 JUDEA, Titus; rev. captive Jew kneeling under trophy; IO ΓΔΑΙΑΣΕΑ.ΙΟΚΥΙΑΕ; fair; v. r.; size, 2d b.
132 SELEUCIA ad Calycadnum, Philip; rev. 2 heads, one with modius ΣΕΛΕΥΚΕΩΝ ΤΨΝ ΠΡΟC ΤΩ ΚΑΛΥΚΑΔΝΩ. Fair, very rare. Size, 1st B.
133 ZEUGMA, Philip; rev. Temple on top of hill; Caracalla; rev. female sitting in temple of 4 columns; Macrinus; rev. temple of 8 columns, side view; Aradus Caracalla; rev. temple of 6 columns; Tripolis, Caracalla; rev. two men standing, one on each side of column. Good, rare. 5 pieces.
134 ANTIOCH, Trebonianus Gallus; rev. Temple; Samosata, Philip; rev. female sitting on rock, at her feet a Pegassus; Seleucia Pieria, Trajan; rev. Jupiter Cacius, in form of a rock, in temple; Commodus; rev. Jupiter sitting; Antoninus Pius; rev. turretted head. Fair, rare. 5 pieces.
135 PHILIP, Antoninus Pius, Trajan, Caracalla, and one other. Poor, rare. 5 pieces.
136 TRAJAN, Philip, etc. Poor, same rare. 9 pieces.

Roman Colonial—Copper.

137 BERYTUS, Heliogabalus; rev. Neptune seizing Amphitrite; Col, Jul. Aug. Fel. Ber. Very fine and rare. Size, 1st B.
138 ANOTHER, nearly similar to 137. Equally fine.
139 SIDON, Heliogabalus; rev. three military standards; Aur, Pin, Metro, Sidon. Very fine and rare. Size, 1st B.
140 BERYTUS, Heliogabalus; rev. Neptune standing in temple of 4 columns, crowned by Victory, standing on pillar; Col, Jul, Aug, Fel, Ber. Very fine and rare. Size, 1st B.
141 ANOTHER; nearly similar in all respects to 140.
142 BERYTUS, Heliogabalus; rev. Fawn standing in temple of 4 columns. Good, rare. Size, 1st B.
143 SIDON, Heliogabalus; rev. Figure of Astarte in car; Col, Jul, Pia, Met, Sid. Fine, very rare. Size, 1st B.

Addenda.

144 CYRRHESTICA, Philip; rev. Jupiter sitting in temple of 6 columns; at his feet an eagle; ΔΙΟϹ ΚΑΤΑΙΒΑΤΟΥ ΚΥΡΗΟΤΩΝ. Good, rare. Size, 1st B.
145 BERYTUS, Valerian; rev. Neptune standing with foot on prow; crowned by Victory standing on pillar: Antioch, Trajan; rev. S. C. in laurel wreath; Berytus, Julius Caesar; rev. man plowing with two oxen; Antioch, Antoninus Pius; rev. S. C. in laurel wreath, Berytus; rev. figure in temple of 4 columns. Good; rare. 5 pieces.
146 BERYTUS, Tiberius; rev. man plowing wtih 2 oxen; Tyre, Valerian; rev. female sitting on shield, holding Victory; Berytus, Macrinus; rev. wolf and twins; Antioch, Trajan; rev. S. C. in laurel wreath; Berytus, M. Aurelius; rev. 2 eagles on standards, within wreath. Poor, some rare. 5 pieces.
147 TYRE, Marcia, Otacilia Severa; rev. basket, in which a shrub is growing; Turiorum; Berytus, Caracalla; rev. temple with 4 columns, in which Neptune stands crowned by Victory; Antioch, Tiberius; rev. S. C. in wreath; Berytus, Hadrian; rev. two eagles on standards; Berytus, Tiberius; rev. man plowing with two oxen. Poor, some rare. 5 pieces
148 BERYTUS, Heliogabalus; rev. Neptune standing with trident and dolphin in temple of 6 columns; Antioch, Trajan; rev. S. C., in wreath; Antioch, Augustus; rev. letters within a circle surrounded by wreath; Antioch, Tiberius; rev. S. C. in wreath; Byblus, Julia Domna; rev. Victory standing. Fair, some rare.
5 pieces
149 TRIPOLIS, Caracalla; rev. temple; Antioch, Nerva; rev. S. C. in wreath; Antioch, Gordian 3d; rev. S. C. in wreath; Tiberius; rev. Military ensigns; Antioch, Trajan; rev. S. C. in wreath. Poor. 5 pieces.
150 ANTIOCH, Tiberius; rev. S. C. in wreath; Berytus, Gordian 3d; rev. Neptune standing with foot on rock, holding dolphin and spear; Hadrian; rev. military standards; Antioch; rev. turretted head; Antioch, Trajan; rev. S. C. in wreath. Some good and rare. 5 pieces.
151 MISCELLANEOUS lot; Sidon, obv., veiled and turretted head of city; fine; rev. Astarte in car; poor, very rare. Antioch, veiled and turretted head; rev. altar with bands; fair. Abgarus, king of Edessa, and Gordian 3d; obv. head of Gordian; rev. head of Abgarus; poor, rare. Augustus; rev. name in wreath; poor. Augustus; rev. S. C.; poor. Ptolemies, 8 and 9, head of Jupiter Ammon; rev. 2 eagles, standing; poor. Arcadius; 3 B., poor. Honorius; 3 B.; poor. Berytus, Antonomous; obv. cornucopia; rev. prow; good;

size, 3 B. Tyre; obv. veiled and turretted head; rev. Victory on galley; in field, monogram of Tyre; fair; size, 3 B. Constantius 2d; obv. veiled head of Concord; rev. figure standing; poor; 3 B. Aurelian and Vabalathus; obv. head of Aurelian; rev. head of Vabalathus; fair; 3 B, rare. 2 other coins; 3 B, poor. 14 pieces.

152 MEDALLION of Antoninus Pius and Marcus Aurelius, laureated head of the former, and bare head of the latter; Greek legend, perfectly patinated and sharp; a rare and valuable piece.

Roman Imperial Coins.

GOLD.

153 Philip I. The Arabian; Stater, or Aureus of Electrum. Pierced; very good and excessively rare.

154 CONSTANTIUS II. Head with fillet of pearls; rev. GLORIA REI PVBLCAE. Two females seated, one with turretted, the other with helmeted head, between them a shield. VOT XX. MVLT XXX., in ex. S, M.N.C. Pierced; very fine, rare.

155 VALENTINIAN, bust with paludamentum and diadem'd head; rev. RESTITVTOR REIPVBLICAE. Soldier with the Labarum and victory. Struck at Antioch; very fine and rare.

156 —— Same; rev. similar, but with monogram in field; rare and interesting, as fine as last, but pierced.

157 Theodosius Magnus. Bust facing with paludamentum and cuiras; a sceptre over his shoulder; rev. Concord seated, in field, a star. CONCORDI AVGGG, in ex. CONOB. Extremely fine; rare.

158 —— Same. Different reverse and pierced. VOTXXX MVLT XXXX.

159 ANASTASIUS. Diademed head, to r; rev. Victory walking to r. In field monogram of Christ. Good and very rare.

160 JUSTINUS. Armed bust, full face with sceptre; rev. Victory standing front face with hasta and globe, surmounted by a cross; struck at Constantinople. Fine and rare.

161 JUSTINIANUS. Armed and helmeted bust, full face, in right hand globe and cross; rev. Victory marching with cross and monogram of Christ in right hand; globe with cross in left; star in field. Very fine and rare.

162 PHOCAS. Bust full face, head diademed and sur-

Addenda.

mounted with a cross; in right hand a cross; rev. Victory standing full face, similar to the reverse of Justinianus. Extremely fine; rare.

163 LEO. Armed, full face bust, resembling that of Theodosius Magnus (No. 157); rev. Victory to l., with long voided cross made of stippled lines. Extremely fine; rare.

164 CONSTANTINUS. Pogonatus (with long beard), bust full face; in right hand globe, surmounted by a cross; rev. cross on four steps. Extremely fine (beautiful), and rare to excess.

165 —— Same. Obv. busts of two emperors (Pogonatus and Heraclius); rev. similar to last. Equally fine and rare.

166 —— Same. With his brothers, Heraclius and Tiberius. The three emperors standing, all armed; rev. cross on 4 steps; in field Greek symbols and letters. Very fine and extremly rare.

167 Another and different Constantine without beard; rev. two standing figures, a cross between them, with loop, and pierced. Otherwise fine.

168 Cup-shaped large Coin of MICHAEL VII. DUCAS. Obv. bust, full face, diademed, holding in the right hand the labarum, in the left a globe with cross. MIX-AH-NASIA; rev. bust of Christ, full face, with nimbus. See Wellenheim, 16,434, where a similar coin is described and ranked rare to the fifth degree. Extremely fine, with a very small pin-hole for loop.

169 Similar Coin of another Emperor, name uncertain. Fine but pierced.

Roman Family Coins—Denarii.

170 ANTONIA. Obv. galley; rev. standards; Leg. XVIII. LVBIC. Good; rare.
171 CALPURNIA. Obv. head of Apollo; rev. horseman. Good.
172 LUCRETIA. Obv. head of sun; rev. crescent and stars. Fair; rare.
173 MINUCIA. Obv. head of woman with helmet; rev. two soldiers fighting over another. Good; rare.
173* PAPIRIA. Obv. head of Rome; rev. Jupiter in quadriga. Fine.

Imperial Denarii.

174 TIBERIUS. Tribute money. Fine.
175 VESPASIAN. Rev. column with statute on top. Good; rare.
176 —— Poor, one pierced.   2 pieces

177 VESPASIAN. Fair. 3 pieces
178 DOMITIAN. Fair, rusted. 2 pieces
179 TRAJAN. Fine. 3 pieces
180 —— Fair; one pierced. 3 pieces
181 HADRIAN. Good; one pierced. 3 pieces
182 ANTONINUS PIUS. Good.
183 —— Imp. Greek of Cæserea Cappadocia; rev. Mount Aregus. Poor, rare. Didrachm.
184 FAUSTINA the Elder. Fine. 2 pieces
185 MARCUS AURELIUS. Two pierced; fair. 4 pieces
186 SEPTIMUS SEVERUS. Good. 2 pieces
187 JULIA DOMNA. Good. 2 pieces
188 GETA and CARACALLA. Good. 2 pieces
189 JULIA MÆSA and HELIOGABALUS. Good. 2 pieces
190 GORDIAN 3d. Good.
191 —— Poor. 2 pieces
192 PHILIP. Fair.
193 ETRUSCILLA. Fair.
194 GALLIENUS. Pierced; poor.
195 FAUSTA. Fair; very rare.
196 CONSTANTINE II. Poor; rare.
197 LEO II., Quinarius. Good; very rare.

Imperial Copper.

198 DOMITIAN, Paduan. Fine; 1st b.
199 " rev. S. C. in crown. Good; 1st b.
200 GORDIAN III.; patinated. Fine; 1st b. 2 pieces
201 " Fine; 1st b. 2 pieces
202 TRANQUILLINA, imp. Greek. Poor; very rare; 1st b.
203 ALEXANDER, Severus, and Philip. Good; one very rare; 1st b. 3 pieces
204 HERENNIUS Etruscus and four others. Fine; 2d b. 5 pieces
205 PHILIP and four others. Good; 2d and 3d b. 5 pieces
206 ANTONINUS Pius and five others; one with two heads. Fair; 1st and 2d b. 6 pieces
207 GALBA and ten others; one with two heads, Caracalla and Geta. Poor; 1st and 2d b. 11 pieces
208 VALERIAN and nine others. Poor; 1st and 2d b. 10 pieces
209 GORDIAN and thirteen others. Poor; 1st and 2d b. 14 pieces
210 MAXIMIAN, etc. Fine; 2d and 3d b. 5 pieces
211 LICINIUS, etc. Fine; 2d and 3d b. 5 pieces
212 CONSTANTINE, Helena, etc. Fine; 3d b. 7 pieces
213 CONSTANTIUS, etc. Fine; 3d b. 6 pieces
214 NUMERIAN, etc. Good; 2d and 3d b. 7 pieces
215 CARINUS, etc. Good; 2d and 3d b. 5 pieces

Addenda.

216 CARUS, etc. Good ; 2d and 3d b.   5 pieces
217 NUMERIAN, etc. Good ; 3d b.   5 pieces
218 ARCADIUS, etc. Good ; 3d b.   5 pieces
219 PROBUS, etc. Good ; 3d b.   5 pieces
220 FLACCALA, etc. Fair ; 2d and 3d b.   10 pieces
221 CARINUS, etc. Fair ; 2d and 3d b.   10 pieces
222 MAXIMINUS, etc. Fair ; 3d b.   10 pieces
223 THEODOSIUS the Great, etc. Fair ; 3d b. 10 pieces
224 Poor ; 3d b.   20 pieces
225 Poor ; 3d b.   20 pieces
226 Poor ; 2d and 3d b.   20 pieces
227 Poor ; 2d and 3d b.   20 pieces
228 Poor ; 3d b.   20 pieces
229 Poor ; 3d b.   20 pieces
230 Poor ; 3d b.   25 pieces
231 JUSTIN I.; obv. bust ; rev. M. between stars. Fine ; 1st b.
232 ANASTASIUS. Fair ; 3d b.   2 pieces
233 JUSTIN II. and Sophia ; figures sitting ; rev. M. Fair ; 1st b.

Miscellaneous.
Greek Silver.

234 PHILIP Epiphanes of Syria ; obv. diademed head ; rev. Jupiter sitting holding Victory. Tet. Fair ; rare.
235 ALEXANDER Magnus. Drachma. Good.
236   "   "   Poor.
237 ARADUS ; obv. bee ; rev. stag and palm tree. Drachma. Poor.

Greek Copper.

238 DEMETRIUS II.; Amisus ; Seleucia Pieria, two coins different reverses ; Alexander Magnus ; Antioch, Imp. Greek of Trajan ; obv. head Trajan ; rev. head City, and one other. Two poor ; others fair.   7 pieces
239 JUDEA ; obv. NEPWNO ; rev. ear of corn, KAIC . . . Poor ; rare.   Size, 3d b
240 Two medieval, and one other ; base silver. 3 pieces

Byzantine Copper Coins.

241 ANASTASIUS ; obv. bust Emperor ; rev. M., above cross. Good.   Size, 2d b
242 ANASTASIUS ; obv. bust ; rev. M. Poor ; 1st b.
243 JUSTIN I.; obv. bust ; rev. M., with star on one side and crescent on other. Good ; 1st b.
244 JUSTINIAN I.; obv. head ; rev. M. Poor ; 2d b.
245 TIBERIUS II.; obv. crowned bust, full face ; rev. XXX above cross. Fine ; 1st b.

246 TIBERIUS II.; obv. crowned bust, full face; rev. M. Good; 1st b.
247 Another, nearly similar to 246.
248 TIBERIUS II.; obv. crowned bust, front face; rev. M. Good; 1st b.
249 MAURITIUS; obv. crowned bust, front face; rev. M. Good; 1st b.
250 Another, nearly similar to 249. Good; 1st b.
251 MAURITIUS; obv. crowned bust; rev. K. Poor; 2d b.
252 HERACLIUS; obv. Emperor standing holding long cross in one hand and globe with cross in the other; rev. M. Poor; 2d b.
253 JOHN ZIMISCES; obv. bust of Christ with nimbus; rev. IHSVS XRISTVS BASILEV—BASILE. Fair; 1st b.
254 ROMANUS II.; obv. crowned bust; rev. RWM EN ΘEW BASILEVS RWMAIEN in four lines. Poor; very rare; 2d b.
255 MAURITIUS and nine others. Poor; 1st and 2d b. 10 pieces
256 JOHN ZIMISCES and nine others. Poor; 1st and 2d b. 10 pieces
257 ANASTASIUS and nine others. Poor; 1st and 2d b. 10 pieces
258 " " " " 10 pieces
259 TIBERIUS II. " " " 10 pieces
260 ANASTASIUS " " " 10 pieces
261 TIBERIUS " " " 10 pieces
262 JOHN ZIMISCES " " " 10 pieces
263 ANASTASIUS and nine others. Poor; 1st and 2d b. 10 pieces
264 JUSTINIAN and nine others. Poor; 1st and 2d b. 10 pieces
265 TIBERIUS II. and nine others. Poor; 1st and 2d b. 10 pieces
266 ANASTATIUS and nine others. Poor; 1st and 2d b. 10 pieces
267 ANASTASIUS and nine others. Poor; 1st and 2d b. 10 pieces
268 ANASTASIUS and nine others. Poor; 1st and 2d b. 12 pieces

Addenda.

Miscellaneous.

269 MISCELLANEOUS. Poor; some rare; 2d and 3d b.
    10 pieces
270 Miscellaneous. Poor; some rare; 2d and 3d b.
    13 pieces
271 GREEK Imperial Tetradrachm of Caracalla. Fine.
272 — Copper and Potin, with others of a mixed character. All ancient.   25 pieces
273 Indifferent ancient copper coins.   50 "
274 Similar lot.   50 "
275 Similar to last.   50 "
276 Similar.   50 "
277 Similar.   150 "
278 Similar.   150 "
279 Closing lot.   165 "

Phoenician Copper Coins.

[This neglected class of coins is really one of the most interesting of antiquity. It is true we are here less frequently, than on those of the Greeks and Romans, brought in contact with familiar historical names and incidents, but we see on these coins symbols of the commercial genius which characterized this nation of Merchant-Princes, as well as evidences and illustrations and that idolatrous religion about which we read so much in the Bible.]

280 BERYTUS (Beyront); head; rev. dolphin on a trident; rev. female on a prow; rev. Neptune standing, etc.
    6 pieces
281 SIDON; head of Elegabalus; rev. idol in a holy cart; rev. Astarte in a similar cart; rev. prow, etc. Larger size.
    4 pieces
282 PHOENICIAN Coin, with the usual emblems of navigation; rev. two Persians (known by their hats) in a biga; undoubtedly very rare and valuable, with others, representing Astarte in her temple, on a galley, and in other situations.   6 pieces
283 TURRETTED head; rev. Astarte on a galley, same on a prow; rev. palm tree, etc.   6 pieces
284 HEAD; rev. sacred bull, and other types.   6 "
285 RADIATED head; rev. owl, same head; rev. eagle, head of Demetrius; rev. galley; probably all, certainly the last, of Tyre.   3 pieces
286 Others, equally characteristic; small and middle size; one with a large cross and palm tree.   12 pieces
287 Similar lot.   7 pieces

HALF SHEKEL.

JEWISH COINS.

288 SHEKEL SIMEON; obv. branch or rod with three stems terminating in buds; Samaritan legend, "Jerusalem the Holy;" rev. a chalice and legend in same character; "shekel Israel Anno Secundo," nearly black; silver of fair quality, in most excellent preservation, and of the highest variety.

289 Alexander I.; star of 8 points; rev. anchor, small; Copper, in fine preservation.

[Only one type extant; [first published by De Saulcy. See Madden, p. 72.]

290 Agrippa II., umbrella or tent? rev. three heads of barley, Samaritan ins., Anno 6; very fine; small copper coin. rare.

291 Same; another equally fine and rare. 8 pieces
292 Another, misstruck. Fine.
293 Same, with one of Alexander I. 2 pieces
294 Bunch of grapes; rev. helmet; palm branch; rev. Nero and one of Agrippa; valuable lot. 3 pieces
295 Vine; rev. Diota (Tiberius); branch of palm; rev. palm tree; and three ears of barley; rev. tabernacle. 3 pieces
296 Palm tree; rev. palm branch; (Augustus after the expulsion of Archelaus; (see Madden, p. 136); with one of Tiberius bearing a well-defined *litnus*, or augural staff, bent at one end; (see Madden, p. 149.) Rare and valuable. 3 pieces
297 OTHERS of Augustus, one of Herod I., and one of Tiberius of a different type. (See Madden, p. 11-15.)
4 pieces
298 Coins of Agrippa II.; Augustus, and one in lead, very remarkable. 6 pieces
N E P),
299 Fine Coin of Nero (palm and C O N O and others of the types already described. A valuable lot for a cabinet. 6 pieces
300 Similar lot; Nero, et. al.; fine, very rare; one of Simon, son of Gamaliel; compare with Madden, p. 178.
6 pieces
301 Similar; (without Simon). 10 pieces
302 Similar; some with head of the Procurator. 11 pieces

303 MEDAL; struck in brass, light in color, and of small specific gravity; bearded head, with horn, in the style of Antique representations of Jupiter Ammon; rev. Hebrew ins.; a well-known medal of disputed antiquity, but about which much has been written by Mr. Walsh, whose work the writer has seen, but cannot quote from at the moment of writing. It certainly has been known for 300 years, and was probably struck before the 7th century.
304 Another; slightly different.

Coins of Crusaders.

305 BOEMOND II. of Antioch; helmed and mailed bust; crescent to left, star to right; BOAMVND REX; rev. short cross, ANTIOCHA; crescent in one angle of cross; silver denarius, or penny. Very fine.
306 Coins (silver pennies) of the Boemunds to the VII. (A.D. 1287); in nearly uncirculated condition; all of Antioch. 10 pieces
307 Silver coin of Henry II. of Cyprus, (Groat size, but thicker); obv. the King seated on his throne; rev. cross and small crosses, the full legend on both sides, HENRI. REI, DE JERVSAL'M, ED, CHIPRE; pierced and broken out, otherwise very fine. *Valuable.*
*308 BOEMUND VII. of Tripoli; beautiful coin, same size and metal as the preceding; obv. cross in a ring formed of small arcs; rev. edifice (square) within similar ring; full legend; SEPTIMVS BOEMVNDVS COMES, CIVITAS TRIPOLIS SVRIE; nearly uncirculated. *Very rare.*
309 Copper coin of James II. of Cyprus?; type; Lion and cross, with silver pennies of Boemund III. et. al.
10 pieces
310 Others of this type; (Lion and Jerusalem cross); with silver pennies. 10 pieces
311 Similar lot. 12 pieces
312 DENARIUS; obv. head front face; "Johannes Rex"; rev. "Damieta"; cross, with two annulets (not described), with others not determined, and, although of value, left to the care and industry of the purchaser; with one exception Copper. 14 pieces
313 LION standing to r.; rev. mounted knight. Silver, fine; nearly groat size. 2 pieces
314 GROS Tournoise of Philip of Anjou; crusader; and smaller. (Half-groats and pennies). 11 pieces
315 BOEMOND's pennies. 10 "
316 Similar. 10 "

317 BOEMOND's pennies.   10 pieces
318 Similar.   10   "
319 Similar.   10   "
320 Similar.   10] "

Old Venetian Republic.

321 ZECHINE (or ducat) of Louis Manin, the last Doge, 1789; (compare with Wellenheim, 2984); St. Mark standing, the Duke kneeling, between them long cross; rev. Christ standing, surrounded by stars; SIT. T. XPE. DAT. TV. REGIS ISTE DVCA. Fine and rare.
322 ANT. VENERIO, 1382-1400; silver coin, groat size; the Duke and St. Mark standing; rev. Christ standing. Fine and rare.
323 Similar, with one of Pascal Ciconia (1585), and another. 3 pieces
324 Copper coins of Venice, etc., (one Jewish).   6   "

Turkish and other Modern Coins.

325 GOLD Mohar of India; intrinsic value, $4.
326 SILVER dollar of Egypt. Fine, rare.
327 Other *fine* silver small coins.   10 pieces
328 COPPER oriental coins.   12   "
329 BASE silver coins, large size.   6   "
330 Same, smaller size.   15   "
331 OLD dollar of Holland; (before dates, etc.)
332 SPANISH and Saxon dollars, 1784 and 1792.   2 pieces
333 Same; half-dollar of 1761.
334 SPANISH Quarter Dollars, ordinary.   2 pieces
335 RUSSIAN 15 Kopeck piece, with another of 5 Kopecks.
                                                  2 pieces
336 MISCELLANEOUS Coppers.   13 pieces
337 STATUETTE, or little Idol in Copper, height 2 inches.
338 Box Fragments of Silver Ring Ornaments, and Drachm of Ancient Rhodes.   The lot

Antique Intaglios.

339 JASPER. Head of Jupiter Serapis between a crescent and star. On lower half of same stone an eagle with uplifted wings. Fine.
340 Same. Suit of armor and inscription; flawed; very rare subject.
341 SARD. Man driving a single horse before a two-wheel chariot. Fine.

Addenda.

342 SARD. Helmeted head. Fine color.
343 Same. Fawn and Nymph with a lyre; limpid, inclining to yellow. Fine.
344 Same. Bearded head in a Macedonian hat.
345 SCARABEUS; white steatite, with an enamel coating of same color.
346 CAVO-RELIEVO Intaglio from Egypt, with a Roman head. Female.
347 TERRE-VERT Scarabooid. Square form. Rare.
348 OLD (Medici) Cameo. Nude female on a couch. Oriental onyx. Fine.
349 MODERN. Head of Shakespeare, head of Minerva, and another Intaglio. 3 pieces
350 HEAVILY mounted cameo pin. The Three Graces, old, and well cut on shell.
351 FINE antique Sardonyx ring; Guinea gold. Subject of Intaglio, "Diana."
352 PERSIAN or Indian seal stone; Cornelian.

www.ingramcontent.com/pod-product-compliance
Lightning Source LLC
Chambersburg PA
CBHW030359170426
43202CB00010B/1427